THE CONTRACT

THE CONTRACT

The Journey of Jimmer Fredette
from the Playground to the Pros

PAT FORDE

SHADOW
MOUNTAIN

FREDETTE FAMILY FOUNDATION

Mission Statement:
To support and strengthen families in need by
providing assistance with setting and reaching goals,
realizing dreams, and achieving self-reliance.

Contact: info@fredettefamilyfoundation.org

Visit us at ShadowMountain.com

Library of Congress Cataloging-in-Publication Data
Forde, Pat, 1964–   author.
   The contract : the journey of Jimmer Fredette from the playground to the pros / Pat Forde.
      pages cm
   ISBN 978-1-60907-140-0 (hardbound : alk. paper)   1. Fredette, Jimmer, 1989–
2. Basketball players—United States—Biography.   I. Title.
   GV884.F57 2012
   796.323092—dc23
   [B]   2012019570

Printed in the United States of America
Lake Book Manufacturing, Melrose Park, IL

10   9   8   7   6   5   4   3   2   1

From Jimmer

This book is for my coaches from Glens Falls and from Brigham Young University. You taught me so many things on the court and also, more importantly, how to succeed off the court.

For my family, who never left my side and who encouraged me every step of the way to achieve my goals—especially my older brother, T. J., for your outstanding courage to overcome huge trials in your life.

For all my fans, a special thank-you for your tremendous support over the past few years.

And for my beautiful wife, Whitney. You were there for me at BYU through the good and the bad. You kept me sane and humble through the whole crazy life I was living—you are my rock and my heart. I'm excited to start a new chapter in life with you by my side.

From T. J.

To my family and closest friends, who have always supported me through the ups and downs of my life.

And to my brother, Jimmer, who, without even knowing it, got me through my darkest times of adversity. Your hard work and sacrifice have amounted to so much more than just success on the basketball court. You inspired me to persevere at a time when I didn't think I could. You've done more for me than I could ever put into words, and I know there couldn't be a prouder older brother on the face of the earth. You did it, bro. Contract fulfilled.

CONTENTS

CHAPTER ONE

BOND

This, thought T. J. Fredette, *is a heck of a way to die.*

He was on an airplane, flying west with his family from New York to Utah. They were going to see Jimmer, the baby of the Fredette family, play the biggest game of his college career to date. It was January 3, 2009, and the sophomore guard at Brigham Young University would be starting against the No. 6-ranked team in the country, Wake Forest.

It was an exciting time, but not for the family's middle child. For him, it was excruciating.

The flight was fine. T. J. was not.

"When I had to get on that plane, it was the worst feeling I've ever had," he said. "I thought I was going to die on the airplane."

Just as Jimmer's career was taking off at BYU, T. J. was crashing with a debilitating vestibular disorder that took

1

months to be diagnosed. It severely affected his equilibrium, balance, and ability to function in everyday life. For about a year, T. J. felt so disoriented and dizzy that he rarely left the couch in the family's tiny, aluminum-sided house at 26 Ogden Street in Glens Falls, New York. An active man in his mid-20s, who had been a very good basketball player in his own right, had been reduced to a listless, depressed shadow of his former self.

Standing and walking were arduous tasks. He watched TV when he could, but even that was a chore at times. T. J. kept a pen and paper with him on the couch, and in intermittent moments of clarity he poured out his thoughts in verse. A rap artist with several recorded songs to his credit, he wrote dark lyrics during this time that were rife with despair:

> *This illness is steadily killing me*
> *I wish it would but instead I'm living in misery*
> *There's not a doctor with knowledge equipped*
>   *for healing me*
> *They wish they could touch on the subject*
> *But they're not feeling me*
> *I'm going crazy*
> *If suicide is inside of me*
> *This probably will be my farewell*
> *I'd rather die than be alive and be a waste of*
>   *flesh*
> *Waiting for death . . .*

The only respite T. J. had from his discomfort and depression was watching Jimmer play ball on TV for the Cougars. "It was a distraction that somehow helped lessen my agony," T. J. said. "My little brother was helping me in ways he didn't even know. With the tribulations I was facing in life, it was such a blessing to be able to experience joy for a couple of hours each time Jimmer had a game. It was my only escape, and without it, I don't know if persevering would have been possible for me. I truly looked forward to watching Jimmer's games." The joy of watching Jimmer's games had spurred T. J. to endure the nausea and join his family on the trip west for the Wake Forest game.

"I did not want to miss that game," he said. "God gave me the strength to get there."

Just leaving the house that morning was an ordeal. T. J. told his parents that it felt as though the left side of his body were being pulled to the ground—a common lament during those days.

But there was another factor T. J. was dealing with at the same time as the vestibular disorder. As an adolescent, he had been prone to panic attacks. Combining disorienting balance issues with an onset of anxiety spiked his misery.

When the plane took off, T. J. felt as if his eyes were still on the ground, causing dizziness so extreme that he completely lost his bearings. A migraine-caliber headache also set in, and he thought he might black out. Then there were random adrenaline rushes that came out of nowhere and further confused his nervous system.

"I remember feeling so anxious for T. J. every time the plane went through any dips or turbulence. His symptoms were so severe, all he could do was grip the armrest and hang on," said Kay Fredette, the boys' mother. "I really don't know how we made it to the next gate after we landed to connect to a different flight. T. J. was so pale and unstable, but he has always had a will of iron when he wants to do something."

Once the draining odyssey ended and the Fredettes landed in Salt Lake City, they made their way 45 minutes south to Provo. Jimmer took it from there. He scored 23 points and had nine assists in a close loss to a Wake Forest team that would be ranked No. 1 for a short time later in the season. It was, by all measures, an impressive coming-out party as a major college basketball talent, and the nation got its first significant taste of the kid with the unique name and the unique game.

The distraction of that game was good for T. J. "Jimmer's stellar play took him away from his sickness for those forty minutes," Kay Fredette said, "but there were times that he would whisper to me that he thought he was going to pass out. Of course, that made me very anxious, and I kept looking at him to make sure he was all right. His face was as white as a sheet. Somehow he managed to get through it, but it was a difficult time. I was trying to be excited and happy for Jimmer, but at the same time I was fearful for T. J. and very distressed at his condition."

Said T. J., "The only time I remember being okay was when he was playing. I was so zoned in, I felt as though I was on the court with him. Then as soon as they called time-out, I had to sit down. Everyone is standing up, going crazy, and I'm sitting down with my head in my hands. I feel like God really helped me in those moments."

This was a relationship coming full circle. For years, it had been T. J. lifting up Jimmer—galvanizing him, directing him, encouraging him, exhorting him. Now the roles were reversed.

At its core, this is a story of two brothers from a blue-collar religious family in upstate New York. Jimmer, you probably know about: on June 23, 2011, he was selected in the first round of the NBA draft by the Sacramento Kings with the No. 10 overall pick; he had won seven different awards as the 2011 National Player of the Year in college basketball; he led all of NCAA Division I in scoring, averaging 28.9 points per game; he carried BYU to one of its finest seasons in school history; and he became a national sensation in the process.

He was such a big deal in 2011 that he changed the language. He became both a one-name superstar—while the entertainment world had Bieber, the basketball world had Jimmer—and a verb. In hoops nomenclature, opponents strafed by Fredette's shooting had been "Jimmered."

But to know Jimmer, you must also know T. J.

T. J. Fredette is seven years older than Jimmer and different in many ways. Jimmer is measured in almost everything he says and does; T. J. is glib, extemporaneous, and witty. Jimmer is slow to anger and difficult to lure into a confrontation; T. J. at times possesses a hair-trigger temper. Jimmer was a solid student when the subject matter interested him; T. J. was rarely interested in any academic pursuits. Jimmer was a shooter; T. J. was a distributor.

Their common ground was Jimmer's game and what it would take to maximize it. Toward that end, T. J. served as his childhood roommate, mentor, coach, adviser, motivator, and confidant. He's been more involved on a daily basis in Jimmer's success than any other person—drilling him, advising him, cajoling him, challenging him, lifting him up when he was down, knocking him down when he got too high.

It was T. J. who took Jimmer to play "prison ball." It was T. J. who summoned all his creativity to invent drills that kept Jimmer interested in practicing fundamentals. And it was T. J. who wrote the handwritten contract that to this day remains taped to the wall above Jimmer's bed in the Fredette home:

"I, James T. Fredette, agree on this day, January 27, 2007, to do the work and make the necessary sacrifices to be able to reach my ultimate goal of playing in the NBA."

Jimmer signed the contract, T. J. signed as the witness, and a moment in Fredette family lore was cemented.

As Jimmer's fame spread, the contract became a

prominent part of his backstory. It was mentioned by ESPN on draft night in June 2011 and in just about every feature that was ever written on Jimmer. The contract idea was even stolen and implemented as part of a television plot involving two brothers—the younger one a rising basketball star, the older one his troubled mentor—on the CBS drama *CSI: New York*.

It's easy to understand the Hollywood appeal of the Fredette story. But the tension between the brothers depicted on *CSI: New York* is pure fiction when it comes to Jimmer and T. J. They have taken turns being their brother's keeper.

• • •

The oldest brother story ever told was a fratricide. According to the Bible's book of Genesis, two sons of Adam and Eve were involved in the first murder.

Cain killed younger brother Abel in the field because God favored Abel and Cain was jealous. Thus sibling rivalry was born and became a part of the human condition. It has been a recurring phenomenon throughout history, a problematic family dynamic that almost everyone has had to deal with in some form.

Not the Fredettes. Not between Jimmer and T. J., even though the younger son went on to far eclipse the older in the sport both of them chose. If ever there were an opportunity for sibling rivalry to fester, this would have been it. But it didn't happen.

"I've always just been so happy for him, to see everything he's accomplished," T. J. said. "There has never been any jealousy, just frustration at myself for not being able to get to where I wanted to be."

Said Jimmer: "He's almost like a father figure to me. He was proud of everything I did. If we were closer in age, we would have fought a lot more, been a lot more competitive, and been on the same teams, probably. It's more like he was watching a son."

To this day, T. J.'s customary greeting to his little brother is a brush of the back of his fingers against Jimmer's cheek. It's been that way since February 25, 1989, when T. J. went to the hospital to meet his newborn little brother. T. J. affectionately touched Jimmer's jowly face and the bonding began.

"I was in first grade, and I remember they called me down to the office and said, 'Your brother was born,' and I got out of school," T. J. recalled. "I was really excited to get out of school. He had a little ski hat on, big cheeks. I kept touching his cheeks. That's almost like our hello, me giving him a tap on the cheek."

Until that day, T. J. had been the youngest in the family, having arrived two years after sister Lindsay. Now the older boy had someone to dote on.

As a small boy, chubby-cheeked Jimmer returned the affection by following big brother everywhere. When T. J. went outside to shoot baskets on the makeshift court in the backyard, Jimmer tagged along. When T. J. started playing organized sports, Jimmer was always the team's water boy. When T. J. got older and went to Crandall Park to play pickup basketball or traveled south on Interstate 87 to Albany for Amateur Athletic Union games, Jimmer sat on the side of the court and watched.

Most older siblings would tell their kid brother to beat it. T. J. never did. He was happy to have Jimmer as a tagalong and didn't tolerate any of his friends picking on the little guy.

"He loves his family. He's very loyal," Jimmer said of T. J. "He loves the *Godfather* movies for the way family members are totally loyal to each other. They always put each other first. T. J. is also a tough kid—extremely tough. He's gotten into some things that he probably shouldn't have with his friends and fighting and stuff like that. You know, because he's a pretty feisty kid. He and his friends, they're all really feisty, have really short fuses. So, my mom was always worried that they were going to get into trouble. And I was always with them, too. But they would never let anything happen to me, so that's why she was okay with it. She knew T. J. would see that I was all right."

There were fights on the basketball court with other kids, but no serious fights between the brothers. Ever.

T. J. was an outstanding athlete, averaging nearly 25 points per game in seventh grade. But in eighth grade, he woke up one morning paralyzed by fear. As a baby, T. J. had experienced night terrors, but this was more severe. This was a full-blown panic attack, the first of many that would change his adolescent life.

During his eighth-grade year, T. J. estimates he missed 40 to 50 days of school because of his debilitating condition. The attacks subsided for a couple of years after that but returned his junior year at Glens Falls High School. The timing was especially bad for T. J.'s athletic career because he was playing varsity football and basketball. He again missed roughly 50 days of school.

After high school, T. J. went to play basketball at nearby Adirondack Community College and, while living at home, slowly got his panic attacks under control. But there would be no Division I dream come true for him, and no professional basketball career. So he diverted his focus to Jimmer.

"I put my attention on him at a young age because I knew I couldn't get to where I wanted to be," T. J. said. "Jimmer could do anything. I saw right away how good he was and how competitive he was. We'd go to work out, and I'd put more attention on him than on myself. One of us was going to do it, and I knew my time was passing. Jimmer was the one who was going to get it done."

Jimmer, ever the pleaser, was happy to do every drill T. J. concocted. When T. J. had him dribble down a hallway with the lights off, jumping out at Jimmer to throw him off-balance, Jimmer was all in. When T. J.'s idea of toughening Jimmer included pickup games against inmates in nearby prisons, Jimmer never hesitated. When

T. J. wrote the contract, Jimmer signed on the bottom line. He trusted T. J.'s guidance and his own ability.

"He's got a very active mind," Jimmer said. "And it's always thinking of new ideas, always thinking of stuff. So that's why, when we did these drills, there were a lot of unorthodox things that people would never think of. Most people are just generic—dribble up and down the court, do your moves, and keep your head up. T. J said, 'We're going to go in this dark hallway. We're going to have one light at the end, and do all these moves. And you're not going to be able to see the ball. And I'm going to jump out at you every once in a while. Keep your balance—and you just keep going.'

"It still does the same thing for you, but it's just a fun way to do it. Maybe it was a better drill, and maybe it wasn't. But it made it fun, so, I wanted to keep playing. You know what I mean? I wanted to play all the time be-cause it was fun to do that type of stuff. That's the way T. J.'s mind was always working and trying to create things.

"I've always trusted him. He's never done anything to break that trust. That's one thing that he is—always, what-ever he says he's going to do, he does it. With anybody. He hates going back on his word. He absolutely hates it. So he makes sure that if he says he'll do something, he does it. That's something I really respect about him, and I try to learn from him in that manner. I've always trusted him; I've always been around him—and whatever he's told me to do, I knew it was going to be for my benefit. So,

I would do it. And it's always worked out. He's never led me astray."

Years later, it was T. J. searching for guidance. For inspiration. For a just a few hours of relief from the constant dizziness and headaches that had become his daily reality. Al and Kay Fredette watched their middle child waste more than a year of his life on their couch because of his vestibular disorder, which came on when he woke up from surgery to repair a partially torn anterior cruciate ligament (ACL).

"It was tough for Mom and Dad," Jimmer said. "One son is almost to the point where he doesn't want to live, and the other son is on top of the world."

It had been no easy climb to reach the top of the world. Jimmer Fredette was an eternally overlooked and underappreciated talent, doomed by location and profile. He never played basketball at a big enough level to satisfy every doubter.

In high school, Glens Falls was far off the recruiting radar that was primarily focused on New York City and its surrounding areas. Even in upstate New York, players from Albany and Niagara Falls got more attention. Jimmer put up big numbers and led Glens Falls High School to some of its greatest successes, but to the consternation of T. J. and the rest of the Fredette family, those things never captured the fancy of recruiters from major colleges.

That's how Jimmer slipped through the Big East recruiting net and wound up across the country at BYU.

It was a great fit in religious and basketball terms—a Mormon university with an up-tempo playing style. For a scorer like Jimmer, Coach Dave Rose's program fit his strengths.

But success was not immediate, nor was playing time granted without being earned. After a humbling freshman season spent as a reserve, Jimmer forced his way into the lineup as a sophomore, became a star as a junior, and then exploded as a full-fledged scoring phenomenon as a senior.

He didn't just lift up a worldwide fan base with his play, taking a Mountain West Conference school to its greatest sporting heights in decades. That would have been enough, of course—enough to ensure Jimmer's name would live on forever in BYU lore. But more important was the lifting he did at home, for his own family.

"Thank heavens for Jimmer's success in basketball because it pulled us all through some really rough times," Kay said. "Jimmer still doesn't realize to this day how much he helped us all. His success was the shining light that got us through the darkness."

The shining light coincided with an upturn in T. J.'s condition. After a succession of doctors could not identify or treat his ailment, the Fredettes finally found one in Vermont who diagnosed T. J.'s vestibular disorder and got him on the slow, grinding path back to health.

As T. J. began feeling somewhat better and Jimmer began playing better, the older brother reached for his paper and pen and wrote his most famous song to date. It's called "Amazing," and it gained national attention during Jimmer's junior season at BYU. The subject matter is self-explanatory and deeply personal:

It's been 21 years, but back when you were younger
I did everything I could as an older brother
To get you to understand that you were given a gift so with each other we would muster
Up a plan to succeed with one another
There's no wonder you would slowly start to climb to success
But it wasn't easy—working hard
Was something that we would stress
So I pressed and pushed you harder
Because you really impressed me when you told me that you wouldn't stop till you were the best
Oh yes
So how could I let you settle for less
And every time I knocked you down
It was all just a test
But you got back up
I could see the dream was for the taking
When you were only five years old because it was truly amazing!
Remember when the media took notice

*The local hero that you had become, so now the
    focus was to keep you levelheaded*
You were bred to be a superstar
*But the most important thing is that you never
    forget who you are*
*Be true to your heart . . . newspaper headlines
    every day*
*TV interviews and radio stations coming your
    way*
*The scouts all over the country flying in to watch
    you play*
*MVP awards, trophies galore, and it made me
    say*
*You were doing great, but this is only the
    beginning*
*Don't be satisfied—we have to try to live out the
    dream*
We need to magnify the talent that you have
Take it further and further
*And every time we tasted glory we worked harder
    and harder . . .*
*You worked your way to see the national atten-
    tion that you needed*
The D1 level
*Where you have succeeded at a level all the
    jealous people said*
That you would never see
As for me

There's no way in the world that there could ever
    be a prouder older brother
They said that you were too white
They said that you were too slow
But we continue to fight and ignite
The type of fire that had you practicing nights
When everybody was partying
You were keeping your sights on the dream, the
    NBA
I'll never forget the day when I wrote you a
    contract that would say
That you would pay
Whatever price
You looked at me with fire in your eyes
Wrote your name upon the line
A defining moment in time . . . now it's time.

Jimmer's time came at just the right time for his stricken brother. A recovering T. J. said, "I've got something to live for."

CHAPTER TWO

YOUTH

Al Fredette moved a framed picture in the family room on Ogden Street to reveal one of the home's many battle scars: a patched-over hole where Jimmer's feet went through the wall one day. He was a toddler Tarzan, wearing nothing but a diaper and swinging on the handle of a chain his mother had bolted to the ceiling when he overdid it and crashed into the wall.

A chain hanging from the family room ceiling won't be found in a Martha Stewart guide to stylish home décor. But in the real world where Kay Fredette lived with her endlessly active youngest child, she reasoned that it would help keep him entertained indoors during bad weather and while she was busy around the house. She envisioned a more placid back-and-forth swing, but rambunctious Jimmer became a kamikaze trapeze artist on it.

Outside, there is more evidence of the Fredette boys'

energetic childhood: the aluminum siding of the house is dented all over from being battered with baseballs, Wiffle balls, kick balls, basketballs—and occasionally bodies. There was a zip line in the backyard for a while and a trampoline, too.

"They broke every window in the house at least once," Al said.

They had help. The Fredette home was *the* place in the neighborhood for kids to congregate, which is far more a testament to its inhabitants than to its creature comforts. It's a tiny house, with just two bedrooms for the five family members to share, and sloped ceilings upstairs that make standing up straight a challenge for full-grown adults. It takes about two strides to get from one side of the family room to the other.

But the cramped quarters never kept anyone away, and the Fredettes never turned anyone away. What little they had, they shared enthusiastically with any and all visitors.

"My parents were so generous and compassionate to people while we were growing up," said Lindsay Fredette, oldest of Al and Kay's three children. "They taught us to let people in."

The Fredettes didn't just let people into the house. They let them into the family.

A teammate of T. J.'s from Adirondack Community College once stayed in the basement for about two months. Another friend of the boys did the same when he encountered difficulties in his home life. Several times Al or Kay would be in the basement doing something when a friend's head would pop up from under a blanket, and they'd have to lecture T. J. yet again: "Tell us when you're inviting someone to sleep over—and tell us how long they're staying." Jimmer estimates that about a dozen of the boys' friends spent time living at the Fredettes' house at one time or another.

"We should've had everyone who stayed sign the walls down there," Kay said.

In a house without much space, there still was always room for someone who needed it. The only things Al and Kay Fredette had in abundance were generosity, empathy, and love for their kids.

"We were their life," said Lindsay. "That's what their joy came from."

Al Fredette worked for six years at Finch Paper Mill, down by the Hudson River in Glens Falls. It is the biggest employer in a blue-collar town that sits on picturesque land at the foot of the Adirondack Mountains. It was mostly dull, occasionally dangerous work that led to a handful of employee deaths. To better provide for his family, he left the mill and became a financial planner, but his life centered more on church and family than on work. Al's energies were directed more to how his kids were living than what he was doing for a living.

"I've always really looked up to him, put him on kind of a pedestal," Lindsay said. "He's kind of been my hero. You learn more about your parents as you get older. You realize some of the things they sacrificed for you that you didn't know about. My childhood was just so magical. My dad went through a lot of struggle—we had some financial struggles and some things—and even though I know he was under so much stress with work and with paying the bills, he would always come outside and play with us when he got home from work.

"He'd play this one game called Monster. He'd come out the door, and we'd all hide and start chanting, 'Monster! Monster!' And you know he was dead tired, but he'd come out the door and go, "Rawr!" and run after us. So, he was always the playful one. I just always saw him being really compassionate to people and accepting people for who they were. He was always really supportive and willing to accept us. He was never one of those fathers who was really harsh on his children and wanted them to be a certain way. He just helped us blossom."

Al has an equally enthusiastic and big-hearted parental partner in Kay. She was a substitute teacher for years but did not take a full-time job so she could concentrate on raising her own kids. Whatever activity they were into, she was into it with them. Whenever one of her children leaves for an extended time, tears are always part of the equation for Kay. That's just the way she's wired. But don't mistake sentimentality for softness.

The boys had a long leash in terms of playfulness and activity—long enough for a chain hanging from the family room ceiling. But Kay drew a hard line when it came to acting the right way toward each other and toward their friends and peers.

"She is a loving lady, but she can be very stern at times," Jimmer said. "She was definitely a disciplinarian if we did something wrong. She was constantly yelling my name and T. J.'s name outside if we were doing something wrong.

"If we started to fight with each other that would definitely bring something out in her. We always had neighborhood kids in our backyard, and we would play every kind of game you could think of. It would get very competitive, and we would yell, and then she would yell at us."

Kay had grown up in an athletic family. Her father, Clinton Taft, was a longtime physical education teacher, coach, athletic director, and principal at Whitehall High School. He coached every sport at one time or another— and sometimes coached two sports at once. His three sons all became physical education teachers and coaches themselves.

Though there weren't a lot of team sports available for girls at the time, that didn't stop Kay Taft from being very athletic and highly competitive. She found an outlet playing tennis but also was happy to be part of whatever the men in the family were doing.

"My whole life was consumed with sports," she said. "When we were in elementary school, the gym that my father worked at was literally right across the street from our house. I practically grew up in the gym because we would go over there to see him every day in his office and the gym and help with anything he needed help with. I handed out uniforms and had my picture taken with the teams every year. To this day, I still love everything about being in a gym—the smell, the locker rooms, watching practices, the squeak of the sneakers, the cheering crowds, and all the other excitement that goes on in a gym.

"I think I have watched more sports than just about anyone out there. I watched my father play with the kids in his Phys Ed classes, I watched him coach all of those years, and I watched all the games my three brothers played and also the games they coached. I watched my husband's games all through the years, I watched the games of all three of my kids in all different sports, and I'm still watching."

According to family lore, Clinton Taft was once walking in the hall of Whitehall High when he heard a ruckus coming from a group of kids in the gym. Concerned that a fight was breaking out, he walked into the gym to find his adolescent daughter, Kay, locked in combat, arm wrestling against the boys. And winning. Kay later accounted for her success by saying, "I had good technique."

"She was feisty, and she still is," Lindsay said. "You don't want to get in her way. She's sweet, she will do anything for anyone—but if you mess with her, she's not going to back down, that's for sure."

Because of the way she had grown up, Kay Fredette had a high tolerance for high-energy children and the games they played—particularly the boys. In her world, kids were not meant to be docile, inactive creatures. That's why the house on Ogden Street was where the action was for all the neighborhood youth.

"She didn't really care if we wrecked things because we didn't really have nice things anyway," Jimmer said. "And she made a rule when we were younger that we could dribble a ball in the house. We could do whatever we wanted in the house. She wanted it to be free and wanted us to stay active and wanted us to stay in sports and everything—it's better than just sitting there and playing Nintendo or something. She wanted us to do stuff."

What the boys did most, of course, was play basketball.

The biggest draw to the house on Ogden Street was the hoop Al put up on one side of the backyard. He and a buddy poured the concrete for the court on a 100-degree day, and a culture was born. Day and night, snow or sun, the Fredette boys and their friends were playing basketball.

Al, who had played basketball in high school and developed a reputation for fanatical effort and intensity, often joined in. Growing up, he was the exception in a household of boys who were not wired in to team sports. Al loved playing high school basketball so much that he would hitchhike to practice from the family's home outside Whitehall, New York, and then have to finagle rides home after practice.

He had a nice hook shot but rarely used it. Al was a

dirty-work player at Whitehall High School—playing tough defense and rebounding and passing the ball to a hotshot scorer named Jimmy Taft. It was a nice way to get in good with the Taft family, since Al wound up marrying Jimmy's sister, Kay.

The great family irony is that Al—virtually forbidden to shoot in high school—would raise a couple of prolific scorers. T. J. often led his teams in scoring while he was growing up, and Jimmer has put his name in record books at all levels for his ability to put the ball in the basket.

And it all began on that hoop in the backyard. That's where Al first coached his boys on the fundamentals of the game and then where T. J. coached Jimmer.

In the winter, T. J. would keep the fun alive by playing basketball on his knees against a very determined young Jimmer on a Little Tykes basketball standard in the cellar. That introduced Jimmer to the challenge of playing against older boys, and then they moved outdoors to the backyard setup. When a half-court game wasn't enough anymore, Al and Kay added a second hoop at the other end of the backyard.

Al put a third hoop on the other side of the yard, and a highly irregular full court was created. There was some cement over here and over there, with a bit of grass and dirt in between. When the weather was hot and dry, the court became a dust bowl. When it was wet, it became a mud pit. Neither condition interrupted play.

"It was a tough place to play, but it was a blast," T. J.

said. "Sometimes we had 20 kids out there. It was *the* place to play."

Even though Jimmer was seven years younger than T. J., he always wanted to join in the games organized by his big brother. "Can I play?" became the unofficial soundtrack that accompanied every activity involving T. J. and his friends. Inevitably, Jimmer would wear them down and wheedle his way into whatever was going on.

"He would always just stand and watch," Lindsay said. "Then you'd look back and he'd be a couple feet closer, and then you'd look back and he'd be a couple feet closer again, and a couple feet closer. He just would inch his way in, and all of a sudden he'd be holding the ball. I don't know how he'd do it, but he was just this charming, cute little guy who could always find his way in."

Once he worked his way into the backyard basketball games, the family created a Jimmer Rule to make things fair: when the chubby seven-year-old with the humorously high-pitched voice was outside what was considered the paint, the bigger boys couldn't guard him. If he ventured into the paint with the ball, they were free to block his shot.

So Jimmer perched outside the paint and called for the ball. Before long, he was making long-distance shots. After a while, he barely missed. The tagalong little brother who was originally considered a liability now became an advantage, and eventually he started being picked first when they chose teams.

"Everybody wanted Jimmer on their team because he'd sit out there and make those threes," T. J. said. "So we had to take out that rule."

In the family history, the discontinuation of The Jimmer Rule marked the beginning of Jimmer's shooting legend.

That legend gained traction in the coming years. When T. J. was on the Glens Falls High School varsity team, Jimmer was the water boy—he was the water boy for every team T. J. played on, in every sport. When T. J. and his teammates would go into the locker room at halftime, Jimmer would grab a basketball and go shoot. Kids were not allowed on the court, but the monitor had a soft spot for Jimmer and let him out there.

It didn't take long before Jimmer's jumpers became an unofficial halftime show unto themselves. Fans were tickled by the curly-haired little kid—still chubby—who was swishing three-pointers from all over. After games, T. J. kept hearing from people raving about his little brother's intermission shooting displays. It got to the point where the team could hear fans cheering for Jimmer through the locker room walls while their coach was trying to go over halftime instructions.

When T. J. wasn't playing, he was organizing backyard tournaments for Jimmer and his friends. He'd help divide up teams, set up brackets, and run the show.

When a tournament was over, T. J. would take his own trophies, put a piece of masking tape over the nameplate on the base, and write in awards for the participants: Most Valuable, Most Improved, Best Sportsmanship—T. J. always had something good to say about everyone who came to play.

"He just has always had a big heart," Kay Fredette said. "T. J. has always cared about other people and tried to make them feel good."

Those people included friends who were struggling, neighbors with disabilities, sporting teammates—and his sister. Lindsay and T. J. were close in age and close in spirit as well. They were best friends growing up.

"I would say that he is one of the most kind-hearted people I know," Lindsay said. "It's funny, for all the struggles and things that he's been through and issues that he deals with in his own head, he is always able to look out and see what other people need. And maybe it's because he's been through things that he's developed a sense of compassion. But he's always helping people, and he is a *magnet* for people. He just has the most magnetic personality.

"For some reason, when people have problems, they go to him. They want to talk to him because he kind of has this sense about him—he knows what to say to people, he knows how to help make people feel better. I didn't always know what was going on with him, but he was always very aware of when I was in need. If I was struggling, even if it was something stupid like I'd just broken up with a boyfriend or something, he was always there to cheer me up and help me get through it. He was my closest friend."

That doesn't mean it's always been a love fest between the two. Not in a family this competitive. T. J., always quick to tag people with nicknames, calls Lindsay "Numbers." That stems from what he calls "The Great Numbers Scandal of '05."

During a spirited family game of Pictionary that year, Lindsay violated game rules by writing down numbers to help her team figure out her clues. After Lindsay's team won the game, the numbers were discovered, and T. J. voided the result and declared that a redo was in order.

"Nobody can make a mistake in this family," Lindsay said, half-joking.

"That was deliberate cheating," countered Jimmer.

"No way that game could end like that," T. J. said.

That is the Fredette family. Content with simple pleasures and a basic lifestyle—but from Pictionary to beauty pageants to the basketball court, competitive in the extreme.

T. J. also was a natural performer. In third grade, he convinced the principal, Mr. Garuccio, to let him do an Elvis Presley impersonation for the school—slicked-back hair, a white jumpsuit, lip-synching to "You Ain't Nothin' but a Hound Dog." You can trace T. J.'s musical performing career back to that day.

Lindsay carved out her own unique performing niche. She danced, played violin in school for eight years, and competed in the pentathlon in track. Her parents attended every track meet, game, recital, and performance in which she participated.

When she was seventeen, Lindsay tried out for the Miss New York Teen USA beauty pageant at the suggestion of her mom, who saw an ad in the paper about it. Despite having no training or experience in pageants, she won.

The original plan was for Lindsay to use her dancing in the talent portion of the competition, but then the family learned there was no talent element in the competition. Lindsay decided to go to the three-day event anyway, which was held in Albany, the state capital. She didn't exactly fit the mold of the beauty pageant veterans: She wore slacks and a sweater while all the other girls wore skirts or dresses on stage.

"I get there and I thought, 'Oh, my goodness. I don't know what I'm doing here. I don't belong here,'" Lindsay recalled. "But there were parts of it that were really fun and parts of it that were just the stereotypical beauty pageant— girls who were really into it and who just kind of made it uncomfortable.

"I remember going into my parents' hotel room the night before the crowning. I just flopped down on the bed and said, 'Mom, I want to go home. I don't want to go tomorrow. Can I just not go?' And she said, 'You're almost done. Just go and just finish it.'"

Finishing it took a long time, because unexpectedly Lindsay kept making the cut, round after round. At the end, the kid nobody had heard of from Glens Falls won the crown. In the back row of the auditorium, a high-pitched victory scream came from Kay Fredette.

"I think the thing that helped me was, since I had no idea of what was coming, I was just completely myself," Lindsay said. "And some of the girls probably do themselves more harm because they're so scripted that they kind of lose themselves, lose their personality, and that comes across as fake. I think my naïveté helped me."

That victory earned Lindsay a berth in the Miss Teen USA pageant in Shreveport, Louisiana, a grueling three-week event in the heat of August. Jimmer and T. J. packed up and went along with Kay for that trip. T. J. enjoyed the buzz of the event—and the girls—but Jimmer was young and bored. The only real highlight for him was getting his picture taken with the guys from the pop musical group *NSync, including one singer named Justin Timberlake. Years later, in 2011, Timberlake would present Jimmer with the ESPY award as the nation's most outstanding male college athlete.

Three weeks away from home was an eternity for all the Fredettes but especially for two boys whose lives revolved around basketball. If they weren't playing in their backyard, they were playing pickup ball all over town. There were games at Crandall Park and East Field, in particular, where they would often spend the day holding the court against all comers.

Those were rough-and-tumble games on the outdoor

courts. One time, a friend's car was stolen from courtside. Many times, fisticuffs erupted. But the important thing to the Fredettes and their friends was the competition.

When altercations broke out, T. J. was frequently in the middle of them. He was an excellent player—a deft passing point guard who could also score. If someone chose to do a little trash talking, T. J. usually had a response. The sharp mind that produces clever rap lyrics now could also produce a barbed put-down for anyone who said something derogatory to him.

And if a teammate got into a skirmish, T. J. would often be the first one who had his back. He takes family and loyalty issues seriously and was never hesitant to jump into a dust-up in defense of his people.

Though he always played hard and was in many rough games, Jimmer never got into any fights. Jimmer was always the problem solver—he never wanted to get into a fight or even an argument with anyone. One reason was that so many of the older kids he played with were willing to defend him. His natural athletic ability was evident early, and the guys he played with and against, and the people who knew him all had a feeling that the kid could someday become something special.

Family friend Chris Shipley has two sons about Jimmer's age and coached all of them in baseball. He got some glimpses of Jimmer's potential in that sport as well.

Jimmer showed up for his first baseball game in high-top sneakers that were untied, with his pants rolled up.

He played shortstop and did just fine without the latest in gear and apparel. Shortly after that, Shipley brought some cleats to the Fredette house for Jimmer, figuring he couldn't afford them. Al Fredette produced a box full of cleats that Jimmer wouldn't wear because he didn't like them.

Jimmer didn't like baseball much and quit when he was twelve. Shipley cajoled him into coming back out to play for his team at age fifteen in a tournament in nearby Saratoga Springs. His recollection of Jimmer's first at-bat in that tournament, after three years away from the sport:

"First pitch comes in, fastball, strike one. Second pitch, curveball, boom, see ya later. Grand slam, 318 feet. Ridiculous. C'mon, hightop sneaker guy.'"

The hightop sneakers were made for basketball, of course, and so was Jimmer. That's where he gravitated and where he succeeded far beyond the expectations of the average kid from a small town in upstate New York.

But the Fredettes have never settled for average and never balked at the improbable. Al and Kay encouraged their kids to think big and think outside the box. A pro basketball player from Glens Falls? A white hip-hop artist? A beauty queen with no prior experience?

Why not?

CHAPTER THREE

FAITH

Hours before the draft on June 23, 2011, the NBA hosted a luncheon at the Westin Times Square Hotel for the 17 players it invited to the green room. Each player had a table of 10 set aside for family members, friends, and agents to join them.

At the Fredette table, the only drinks were water and apple juice. That was in keeping with the family's religious beliefs. The Church of Jesus Christ of Latter-day Saints forbids the consumption of alcohol and other addictive substances, part of a health code known as the Word of Wisdom, designed for healthy living. It's one of the many strictures that make the LDS way of life something of an anomaly to the rest of modern America.

Latter-day Saints believe in abstaining from sex outside of marriage. They believe that a man and a woman can be married for all eternity. They believe the family is central to

God's plan. They put a premium on honesty. They believe that Sundays are holy days, not work days. They believe in repentance, baptism, confirmation, and receiving the Holy Ghost. They take seriously the obligation to tithe their income and donate to charitable causes.

"The bar is set high for a faithful Mormon," says *Mormons: An Open Book,* which Deseret Book Company released in 2012. The book cites a number of statistics and surveys showing that, in general, Mormons are more devout—in terms of attending worship services, reading scriptures, and praying regularly—than the general population. But that book also notes that LDS members do not have "pretensions of perfection or claim that we always fully live up to these standards."

The book quotes late church elder Neal A. Maxwell as saying the LDS church "is not a well-provisioned rest home for the already perfected." In other words, Mormons are not spending a lot of time congratulating themselves on being better than everyone else.

The LDS way of life is not something the Fredettes were born into. It's something they chose.

As a young man, Al Fredette was a seeker, trying to find a religion that fit him. In fact, Kay laughingly refers to Al as "Mr. Theology." That's because he enjoys studying and discussing the doctrines of different faiths.

He'd been raised going to the Baptist church in Whitehall, New York, until the age of 14, and then he pretty well dropped out of the religious scene for a while.

But an older brother, Dennis, enlisted in the service, met Susan, a Mormon girl (even in that meeting the Fredette family enthusiasm for basketball played a role) and joined the LDS church in Germany.

He brought the LDS experience home to upstate New York with him. Soon, others in the family started going to church with him—but Al was not one of them. Finally, Al's sister Bonnie told him it "would mean an awful lot" to her if he would accompany her to an LDS service.

Al went, and he liked what he experienced. Afterward he started investigating the LDS church. He met missionary Kimball Rogers, the future father of Jimmer's BYU teammate Stephen Rogers, and spent hours discussing the LDS faith with him. The more Al learned, the more he liked it—and he liked what converting had done for Dennis Fredette.

Craig, another of Al's older brothers, had been a roofer, working with a group of men who were hard drinkers. They would start drinking beer in the morning and move on to hard liquor by nightfall. After deciding to join the LDS church, Craig quit drinking altogether and also quit his job as a roofer. He found a job with the Glens Falls police department that allowed him to spend more time with his family. The example of his older brothers made a big impression on Al and later became a strong reason for him to seriously investigate the Church.

In the process of finding his own religious path, Al did a lot of reading and studying. He had looked in to a number of Christian faiths. With friends, he'd sometimes attended services at a black Baptist church that occasionally invited an LDS choir there to sing. And he grew up going to Methodist and Baptist churches.

But the LDS teachings seemed to fit him best. He liked the emphasis on family—"Families Are Forever" is one of the tenets of the church—and the socially active atmosphere. And he came to really enjoy the involvement of the members in the operation of the church.

"There's no paid ministry, so you're expected to be a large part of the church itself," Al said. "For 42 years, I've been going to church and had two or three different callings at the same time. I've never had a time when I didn't have a calling."

Among Al's callings were multiple stints as a Sunday School teacher for all different age levels, from adults to young kids, and serving as president of the Young Men Association. He currently serves as a mission leader, working with two young missionaries in their proselytizing efforts. Al has personally baptized a number of people into the LDS faith.

The local congregation of Latter-day Saints is called a ward, and the Glens Falls Ward is geographically vast—Al said it stretches across about 50 miles. (In Utah, by contrast, where the population of Mormons is denser, wards might extend no more than a few square blocks.) With such a far-flung congregation, Al was kept busy driving up to an hour each way to shuttle those without transportation to and from church meetings.

Kay, who was raised Catholic, sometimes attends LDS services. Though she has never formally converted, she saw many of the same positive attributes in the church as Al did.

"It's a family-oriented church," she said. "I knew my kids would get a good idea who Jesus Christ was. I like that about the LDS church. I had no problem with them being brought up in the Mormon faith."

But Al and Kay did not force the LDS faith on their children. Instead, they were given the chance to decide on their own if they wanted to be baptized into the church or find a different route. All independently chose to become LDS during their elementary school years.

Living a Mormon life has helped keep the Fredette kids close to each other and far away from much trouble—but that occasionally led to making some hard choices during adolescence and young adulthood. With Mormons such a small percentage of the population in the Glens Falls area, they mingled with many kids who had decidedly different outlooks—religious and otherwise.

Al remembers tutoring his children on how to handle themselves socially in situations where Mormons—and many others of different religions—would feel uncomfortable.

"I told Lindsay, if you go to a party, and there's something wrong—alcohol, drugs, anything that's not right—you've got to have the guts to call me and come home," Al said. "I told the boys the same thing: if things start to get too crazy, come on home.

"There were times my sons would be home on Friday night because their friends knew, 'We can't invite T. J. and Jimmer to this party.'"

But the Fredettes certainly were not considered a "no-fun" family. The kids never seemed to resent the restrictions on their social life, and it never seemed to cost them much popularity at school. They did things their own way and were respected for it. In return, they did not look down on others who lived life differently.

"The most important thing you're ever going to do in this life is be a good person," Al told his kids. "If your role model is Christ, you're going to follow his example. You can be the best athlete there ever was, but if you're not a good person, nobody will like you."

Attending BYU, the flagship LDS-owned university in Provo, Utah, was a fairly natural outgrowth of the family lifestyle and faith. Al's brother Dennis went to school there, and Al himself studied there for a semester. Lindsay graduated from BYU in 2002, and Jimmer followed.

Al and Kay liked the fact that religion classes were a requirement each semester—some semesters, Jimmer took two. They liked the fact that a high percentage of students attended services regularly. And they liked the fact that the temptations so present on other campuses are largely absent in Provo. All things considered, the Fredettes believe their children made informed religious choices and know what they've gotten themselves into spiritually.

"You have to know what you believe, study what you believe, and ponder it to convert to what your principles and faith are," Al said.

Jimmer, who was married to former BYU cheerleader Whitney Wonnacott on June 1, 2012, follows Mormon doctrine but did not go on a full-time mission as so many other students at the school do.

Even though he did not go on a mission and is in a profession that requires him to work on some Sundays, Jimmer remains a devout and practicing Mormon. He says he prays daily—first thing in the morning, last thing at night, and as needed in between.

"I just pray for strength, to keep everybody safe, and for little things that you're going through during the day," Jimmer said. "For help with adversity."

He has often been compared to former Denver Broncos quarterback Tim Tebow, whose rampant worldwide popularity stems only partly from his football abilities. Tebow's Christian upbringing and willingness to wear his faith on his sleeve has endeared him to those who admire his religious lifestyle. His open display of his faith has also spawned a vast resistance to Tebow from people who claim Tebow's religion was forced upon them or who scoff at any notion that his football success is in any way related to his piety. Many simply don't believe God wants Tim Tebow to win more football games than less-devout players.

Jimmer's practice of his religion has been far less con-
troversial, mostly because it has been far less public. He
has not been seen "Tebowing," or praying on the sideline
during a game. He does not begin every interview with
"a shout-out to Jesus." He is less likely to use his athletic
celebrity as a platform for religious statements.

The similarities come from their status as campus idols
who embraced their religions' beliefs and rejected a lifestyle most others in their shoes would embrace. Neither
young man was looking to score with a different girl every
weekend. They were not partiers armed with fake IDs. If
there were bar fights at their schools, you could be assured
that the names *Fredette* and *Tebow* would never appear on
an arrest report.

Those similarities extended to their public grace and
humility. Tebow is famous for good deeds and for reaching out to the less fortunate. Jimmer has done the same
and has been generous with his time in promoting good
causes—almost to a fault on occasion. Fans are not likely
to be big-timed by either athlete.

Members of The Church of Jesus Christ of Latter-day
Saints can be as proud of Jimmer for representing them
well as Evangelical Christians are of Tim Tebow. Jimmer's
faith is no less important to him—it just won't be as
big a part of his public persona. It's there, but it's also
private.

Jimmer's rise to prominence makes him part of
what *Newsweek* declared in a 2011 cover story to be the

"Mormon Moment" in America. It may seem strange for a religion to become trendy—especially one that is a poorly understood niche presence in many parts of the nation—but the LDS church is currently a topic for serious discussion in politics, entertainment, and popular culture.

According to Pew Center polling, there are 6 million Mormons in America. It only seems as though all of them are in the news lately.

The most prominent Mormon is Mitt Romney, the 2012 Republican nominee for president. Among the Republican rivals he defeated for that nomination is fellow Mormon and former Utah governor John Huntsman Jr. The U.S. Senate is led by Mormon Harry Reid, a Democrat from Nevada.

Other Mormons have been widely seen, read about, listened to, and discussed in the media and Hollywood as well. Before his death, church president Gordon B. Hinckley was interviewed and treated favorably by legendary newsman Mike Wallace, who maintained a warm personal relationship with him. National radio talk-show host Glenn Beck, a Mormon convert, is a daily lightning rod who is beloved by conservatives and reviled by liberals. Popular singer and song writer Gladys Knight converted to Mormonism a number of years ago and has been very open about her adopted faith. Though the LDS church long ago (1890) ceased the practice of polygamy, HBO's series *Big Love* had a five-year run of popularity from 2006 to 2011, chronicling the lives of a contemporary, fictional fundamentalist "Mormon" family that practices polygamy. The Twilight series of vampire romance novels, written by Mormon Stephenie Meyer, were huge worldwide sellers and spawned a succession of box-office movie hits. Well-known LDS athletes include NBA basketball players Danny Ainge (who also played professional baseball), Thurl Bailey, and Shawn Bradley; baseball player Harmon Killebrew; and NFL football players Steve Young, Heisman Trophy winner Ty Detmer, and Austin Collie. There is even a "Jimmer Junior" in the basketball ranks, Chicago high school star Jabari Parker, who was featured in May 2012 on the cover of *Sports Illustrated* in part for his athletic talents and in part for his LDS faith.

Broadway produced its own take on the religion with *The Book of Mormon*, a lively musical about Mormon missionaries that won nine Tony Awards, including one for best musical. Not all depictions of the Mormon religion have been glowing, nor have they necessarily fallen in line with LDS church tenets. Church members may have enjoyed parts of *The Book of Mormon* musical but probably cringed at many others.

In *The New York Times*' glowing review of the play in 2011, it was described as "blasphemous, scurrilous and . . . foul-mouthed. . . . But trust me when I tell you that its heart is as pure as that of a Rodgers and Hammerstein show. . . . 'The Book of Mormon' is about naïve but plucky educators set down in an unfamiliar world, who find their feet, affirm their values, and learn as much as they teach. . . .

"Which brings us, inevitably, to the issue of sacrilege. This show makes specific use of the teachings of the Mormon Church and especially of the ecclesiastical history from which the play takes its title. Church founders like Joseph Smith and Brigham Young appear in illustrative sequences, as does Jesus and an angel named Moroni. When delivered in musical-comedy style, these vignettes float into the high altitudes of absurdity.

"But a major point of 'The Book of Mormon' is that when looked at from a certain angle, all the forms of mythology and ritual that allow us to walk through the shadows of daily life and death are, on some level, absurd; that's what makes them so valiant and glorious."

With the greater public curiosity has come greater scrutiny. When Romney's tax returns for 2010 and 2011 were made public, the sizeable amount of money he had donated to the church prompted a lot of discussion—a total of $4.13 million in those two years alone.

As the *Christian Science Monitor* wrote in early 2012: "A slew of poll results over the past year, from Gallup and the Pew Center to CNN and ABC, have all shown that Americans' attitudes toward Mr. Romney's Mormon faith may play a decisive role in his campaign.

"Now that the strength of his religious conviction has a dollar sign attached to it, the question arises: Will his tithing invigorate the uneasiness that many Americans, including evangelicals and some other Protestants, have toward the Mormon church and its adherents?"

Many Mormons believe that uneasiness is based in a lack of understanding of their faith. Toward that end, and in an effort to capitalize on the recent surge in LDS visibility, the church is trying to educate the uninformed. *Mormons: An Open Book* begins with a list of "Ten Facts to Know When Meeting a Mormon":

1. Mormons are normal people. Your Mormon friend doesn't secretly live in a compound, and he won't arrive at your house in a horse and buggy. He is not part of a cult or an anti-social group. He will be a regular person following his beliefs, just like you follow your beliefs. . . .

2. Mormons believe in salvation through Jesus Christ. Your Mormon friend believes in Jesus Christ and His saving grace, and she or he centers their worship on Him. Having faith in the Lord Jesus Christ is the first principle of her religion, and her religious desire is simply to try to follow Jesus' teachings as closely as possible. . . .

3. The Mormon Church is The Church of Jesus Christ of Latter-day Saints. Your friend is a Mormon, is LDS, is a Latter-day Saint, and is officially a member of The Church of Jesus

Christ of Latter-day Saints—and no, they aren't four different churches. They are all the same thing. . . .

4. Mormons don't worship Joseph Smith. Your Mormon friend believes Joseph Smith was a prophet just like other prophets in biblical times. . . . He doesn't worship Joseph Smith any more than a Catholic worships Peter or a Jew worships Moses. . . .

5. Mormons are nicknamed after one of their books of scripture, the Book of Mormon . . . , which is "another testament" of Jesus Christ's divinity. It is a prophetic record translated by Joseph Smith about a people who lived in ancient America. . . . [Your Mormon friend] also believes in, reads, and studies the Old and New Testaments. . . .

6. Mormons believe in living prophets, and the LDS church has a living prophet, a man currently on earth who your Mormon friend believes to be God's authorized spokesperson, just as Abraham, Moses, and Isaiah were in their day. The prophet is someone whom your Mormon friend greatly respects and looks to as a servant of Jesus Christ [like the Catholics look toward their Pope]. . . .

7. Modern Mormons are not polygamists. Your Mormon friend is not a polygamist. He doesn't have three wives, nor does he believe (or wish!) he should. Faithful Mormons haven't entered into polygamous marriages since the 1890s. . . .

8. Mormon women are not subordinate to Mormon men. . . . Mormon women are independent, highly honored in their role as mothers, have professional careers, think for themselves, serve in leadership positions and in councils in the LDS congregations, and, if married, are equal partners with their husbands in governing their families. . . .

9. Mormons don't drink alcohol, coffee, or tea. . . . Mormons have a code of health they live by, and they try to abstain from anything that could damage their health, impair their judgment, or be addictive or habit-forming—especially tobacco, alcohol, coffee, and tea. . . .

10. Mormons serve as lay ministers in their local congregations. Odds are your Mormon friend has a "calling" within his or her local LDS congregation—something he or she has been asked to do voluntarily and without compensation. Many Mormons give

substantial time each week fulfilling these assignments. . . .

There is, of course, more than just that to know when meeting Jimmer and T. J. Fredette. Faith and family are prime parts of the equation—but so are their roots in up-state New York, a place that helped shape the men they would become.

CHAPTER FOUR

HOME

There is graffiti spray-painted on the tan brick wall of Achenbachs Jewelers in downtown Glens Falls. And the proprietor loves it.

"I'll probably leave it up forever," said Joshua Murphy of Achenbachs.

It's a blue stencil of Jimmer Fredette in a BYU uniform shooting a jumper. Above it, someone has wryly written in black marker, "Who's that?"

Everyone in "Hometown, USA"—as Glens Falls was dubbed by *Look Magazine* during World War II—knows who Jimmer is. Residents of this burg of roughly 15,000, located on the Hudson River about three hours north of New York City and three hours south of Montreal, could not be more proud to call him one of their own.

When he was home a few days before the June 2011 NBA draft, the New York State Senate honored Jimmer. On the night of the draft, Glens Falls held a "Jimmer Jam" at the downtown Civic Center. The city's biggest arena opened its doors to everyone free of charge to watch their favorite son launch his pro career. A display was set up featuring all his National Player of the Year awards, and a Jimmer highlight video was shown.

For residents of a small town, he is the personification of hope. He is the living, local realization that grand goals can be reached from almost any starting point.

"I used to have a teacher in high school who would listen to us talking about sports and say, 'There's never been a kid out of this area make it in sports, so stop dreaming and start studying,'" Murphy said before the draft. "I was thinking today, 'You know what? One is about to make it.'"

Still, the odds are telescopically long. Glens Falls has produced about four really good major league baseball players, a couple of pro hockey players, a pro wrestler, and some winter-sports athletes—but an NBA player? No. Jimmer would be the first.

The town at the foothills of the Adirondack Mountains offers a plethora of outdoor pursuits: skiing and outdoor hockey in the winter, and fishing, camping, and golfing in summer. Legendary Saratoga Race Course, a horse-racing mecca in the summer months, is just 25 miles down the road at Saratoga Springs.

Though the Fredettes, along with Kay's family, the Tafts, went to the racetrack every summer to watch the horses run, they mostly went to the gym and played basketball instead, or to the neighborhood parks in the warm-weather months to play pickup ball.

The challenges at the parks weren't always limited to competition on the court. You had to keep an eye on your car, too. A Fredette family friend got his car stolen once during a pickup game. And the Fredette family car was swiped once when thieves found the keys Al had hidden in the car during the game.

"The car was right there," Jimmer said. "Sometime during the game it was stolen. Probably two hours later, we're done playing ball, and we noticed. We just walked home and called the cops. They found the car four or five days later, ditched."

For young men in this area, the more likely destination than the draft lottery is a job at Finch Paper Mill, where raw logs are converted into pulp and pulp into paper. It is one of the largest employers in town and a place Al also once worked.

Glens Falls is a great place to live, though population declined for five straight decades from 1950 to 2000 before rising again in the last decade. Though many young men from the area end up working at the paper mill, most go away to college. The town has its picturesque features but also its gritty side. Anyone who thinks the Fredettes had a privileged upbringing in some sort of soft surburban setting is mistaken.

"This is a blue-collar town," Jimmer said. "We're blue collar, born and bred."

Success and fame didn't change that. In the days leading up to the draft, T. J. and Jimmer got around Glens Falls in the family's aged minivan. For most of his life, Jimmer's wardrobe consisted almost entirely of sweats and other jockwear. And if you wanted to find the brothers anywhere other than at home, the likely place was Angelina's.

Angelina's is a small, no-frills Italian restaurant owned by the Aunchman family, who are close friends with the Fredettes. T. J. even worked there for a while, and the Fredettes are welcome behind the counter and in the kitchen whenever they visit the restaurant. The Aunchman boys and Fredette boys have even discussed opening an Angelina's in Utah together.

The original restaurant is in a nondescript strip mall not far from a 1700s Quaker settlement that is marked by a historical marker. The marker speaks to the interesting mash-up of ethnicities and faiths in the area.

A site of several battles during both the French and Indian War and the Revolutionary War, the area had large populations of Quakers and French descendants. In later years there was an influx of Irish and Italian workers, many of them Catholic. And the only congregation of The Church of Jesus Christ of Latter-day Saints in the region is located in Glens Falls.

The Fredettes are of French descent. Kay's side of the family is French and Irish. It was Kay's side that imbued their household with a deep love of sports. Al's side also had a love of sports, but their sports entailed going outside their country home and having free-for-all football games and various other sports until they were old enough to join school programs.

Jimmer, in particular, was born and bred for sports. The legacy of athleticism runs deep in his veins and in his family tree.

His full name is James Taft Fredette, and the middle name comes from Kay's side. The Taft family patriarch, Clinton Taft, was a landmark athletic figure in nearby Whitehall, New York, which is about 25 miles northeast of Glens Falls toward the New York–Vermont border.

Clint Taft played football at Whitehall High School under legendary coach Ambrose "Gilly" Gilligan, who in the 1930s helped turn football into the isolated town's bonding agent. That phenomenon was described in 2006 in the *Albany Times-Union*:

"A bonfire touched the sky the night before every game, and on the day of each contest, a 24-piece band with baton-twirlers in billowing red skirts led a parade over the cobblestones of Main Street, across the bridge, to the field by the water.

"Everyone came to the pre-game jamboree, and every store in the village was closed. Up to 12,000 people would turn up, biting their nails and crossing their fingers, to watch the Maroons do battle."

Clint Taft was one of the boys they watched in the '30s,

as Whitehall developed into a power that once put together a 27-game unbeaten streak. His athletic career continued after high school, and Taft was inducted into the Green Mountain College Athletic Hall of Fame in Vermont, where he was a three-sport athlete and still holds a record for heaving the javelin.

But it was what Clint Taft did thereafter that cemented his legacy in the area. Taking the baton from legendary Gilligan, under whom he worked as an assistant coach, Taft coached every sport they had at his alma mater—sometimes multiple sports simultaneously—for 40 years. Kay Fredette recalled days in the spring when her dad was conducting baseball practice at one end of the school's playing fields and track practice at the other end. Then at night, after his coaching duties were finished and he'd eaten dinner with his family, he'd go back to the school and run the adult education programs. In the summers, Taft earned extra money as an iron worker.

Clint was a local sports legend and had opportunities for bigger jobs in bigger towns in his 40s and 50s, but he never took one. He wanted to keep his family grounded in Whitehall. The town reciprocated by treating him like the respected coach and mentor for his teams that he was.

From 1952 to 1954, Taft's football program did not lose a game. During that same span, he also coached the school's basketball and baseball teams, and they were successful as well. Of the nine possible conference championships Whitehall could have won in those three sports from

1952 to 1954, it won seven—and in the other two finished second. All this despite being at a numerical disad-
vantage in terms of enrollment compared to some conference rivals.

When Taft died in 2008 at the age of 88, his family received many letters from former players saying how much
Coach Taft had meant to them as teenagers. A few years
ago the playing fields—"The Playground"—at Whitehall
High were named in his honor.

The Taft house, in close proximity to the school, was a
popular postgame spot for the coaches and their families
to rehash the just-completed competition over dessert. No
wonder the Taft children grew up believing that sports and
education were staples of everyday life.

Clint Taft was a loving father but not prone to excessive
displays of sympathy when things went wrong for his kids.
When one of them lost a game or got hurt or got a bad
grade or was faced with a difficult assignment athletically
or academically, the message was simple:

Don't worry. It'll pass.

His boys—Jerry, Jim, and Lee—were what you would
expect from sons of a coach: multisport athletes who had
leadership positions on their teams and then went on to
become physical education teachers and coaches themselves. In high school, all three were point guards, and two
were quarterbacks.

The Taft boys were not blessed with great height but
were naturally strong and wide-shouldered. They came by

their work ethic and leadership qualities rather naturally. But Lee Taft was the positional black sheep in football, playing running back instead of QB.

He also became the educational black sheep, leaving teaching to train athletes individually to maximize their potential. He left the area for many years, plying his trade in different parts of the country, but he would have a tremendous impact on Jimmer's development.

"He's still my trainer," Jimmer said.

After coaching football, basketball, and track, Lee Taft's first stop outside the traditional school teaching/coaching field was to attend the United States Sports Academy in Daphne, Alabama. After that, he coached strength and speed work at the Bolletieri and Palmer tennis academies in Florida and for the Kentucky tennis program.

Then he moved back to Glens Falls and opened his own strength-and-speed coaching business while also returning to teaching. Before Lee opened his own facility, the workouts were conducted wherever possible: a gym when available, the track at Glens Falls High, the driveway at Lee's house, or even Lee's two-car garage when the snow piled up and the temperatures plummeted and they were forced indoors.

"In the middle of winter, we'd be out there in the garage training," Lee recalled. "In the summer, if there was a flat area, we got the work in."

It was then that Lee began training Lindsay and

T. J.—and, inevitably, Jimmer, the kid who hated to be left out of anything and always worked his way in.

"Kay would always pull him off to the side because he wanted to be in it," Lee said. "We're talking four, five years old. So I started doing some stuff with him."

Said Jimmer: "I always wanted to be involved. There were some things that he'd let me do and then other things he'd say, 'No, you can't do it.' But then I'd be on the sideline, trying to mimic it. I just wanted to do what they were doing."

The roots of Jimmer's deceptive athleticism were put down then, through Lee's unorthodox training regimen.

"We worked on landing," Lee said. "Everybody wants to work on jumping, I worked on landing. I had them jumping off a 4-to-6-inch box and landing in an athletic stance, ready to go in any direction of a jump-stop in triple-threat stance.

"We worked on lateral movement—lateral shuffle, crossover moves, opening your hips. We worked on acceleration—a lot of quick and random change of direction drills. We played catch on one foot and then exploding in a direction.

"It looked kind of crazy, a little goofy, but it was turning the body into a more balanced, more explosive mechanism."

Jimmer became a master of the half-inch offensively in part because he was trained by Lee to make every inch count. Getting off shots in traffic against taller opponents required a mastery of tight spaces. Same with getting enough separation from quicker defenders.

"You don't get beat in 94 feet," Lee said, citing the length of a basketball court. "You get beat in four feet. So we worked on quick change of direction in limited space. It gave him great balance and the ability to hesitate, so he can get a defender leaning one way and then go by him."

Said Jimmer: "It's not about being the most athletic, quickest, or fastest but knowing how to use your body to your advantage, so you can be successful. I can stop on a dime, and that's how I'm able to create the space I need when I shoot the ball. And even if the kid guarding me is really quick, he's going as fast as I am, but then all of a sudden he's going really quick in the other direction and I'm coming back. So, that's the biggest thing for me— being able to quickly change direction. It's all about your center of gravity being exactly where it's supposed to be. We worked a lot on that, with being able to stop and start quick. Being able to stay on balance has a lot to do with your core. He does a *lot* of core work."

Since Lee wasn't training Jimmer for the 40-yard dash or working on his shooting skills—those were developed on their own—they didn't need much room. A tight garage was a perfectly acceptable workout area, and Jimmer was a perfectly voracious pupil for Lee's methods.

With twenty-three years of experience as a trainer, Lee was impressed by Jimmer's unusual determination: "He always wanted to be better," Lee said. "He wanted to be better than the people around him. Jimmer just took to it. Even though he wasn't really fast and quick when he was younger, he had very good feet and very good hand-eye coordination."

Jimmer's latent athleticism was buried beneath a layer of baby fat as a kid. Lee had to tailor his workouts to fit Jimmer's still-developing physique.

"All of a sudden, halfway through his sophomore year of high school, everything started to take off," Lee said. "He grew and lost the baby fat he had. I was able to train him harder. He started dunking and running by people. You can't rush maturity in an athlete. And as he got older, he realized that his skills were pretty good, but to play at the next level he needed to be quicker and stronger."

Lee eventually moved his family and started another speed-and-strength business in New Castle, Indiana, in 2004. Even though he was living in Indiana, he continued to run his first Speed Academy in New York. And he still tutored Jimmer in the fine arts of improving his body when possible. Lee worked him out in the summers when Jimmer was at BYU and sent him workouts when he was in school. "He's trained with me for fifteen years," Lee said. "It's a way of life. It's not six weeks and see you later. Everything I gave him, he got better at. From a young age, he understood what it took to be good."

On the Fredette side of the family, Jimmer and T. J.'s father, Al, also grew up in the same area. He was part of a family of six kids: two girls and four energetic boys. Al passed along a humorous oral history of the mischievous times and hijinks he was involved in with his siblings growing up.

"We lived in a country setting halfway between the towns of Fort Ann and Whitehall," Al said. "There was not much to do, so we had to make our own fun."

Al told stories to his kids and their friends about the many times the Fredette boys used to sneak in the nearby drive-in to lie on the ground and watch the latest feature film. Many people who attended the drive-in used to see the silhouettes of their heads on the screen bobbing up and down in the front.

To make the drive-in adventure more fun, Dennis—the brother Al called "the ringleader"—suggested that they pretend they were burglars about to carry out a top-secret heist. So they all dressed in black and crawled through the tall grass, trying to go undetected as they sneaked in. It was all about the excitement for them. If the activity of the day wasn't exciting and a little bit daring, then the Fredette boys weren't interested.

Another vivid memory Al had involved the Great Meadow Prison—one of the same prisons where Jimmer and T. J. would later play basketball against some of the inmates. Growing up, Al and his siblings lived only a couple of miles from it. It now has a medium security prison there as well as the maximum security, but at the time Al's family lived near it, the entire facility was maximum security.

Al remembers one time when there was word that an

escapee was on the loose from the prison. Coincidentally, the Fredette boys were alone at the house that day. Sure enough, a knock came at the door. Al can't prove it, but he was sure it was the escapee trying to find a place to hide. The escapee got a good view into the house as he was standing at the front door, and fortunately Al's older brother Dennis, who was about 15 years old at the time, was there cleaning a rifle from their gun collection. The escapee took one look inside the house and decided it wasn't the place he wanted to try to take refuge. He promptly ran off the front porch. That story never failed to pique the interest of Al's kids, along with that of their friends.

Al also told his family about one summer day when their mischief turned into a big scare. The boys and one of their friends decided they would throw stones at the semis that rolled by on the main highway in front of their house. They aimed at the trailer, not the tractor up front where the driver was, and the competition was to see who could hit a trailer first. The family friend who was visiting managed a strike—but hit the tractor, not the trailer. Luckily the stone didn't break the glass and the driver wasn't hurt, but to the boys' surprise and horror, the driver screeched to a halt. Bringing the big rig to an abrupt stop led to its jackknifing across the road and tying up traffic, but that didn't stop the driver. He climbed out of the truck and ran up the hill after the boys, and Al said he was never so scared in his life.

When their father learned of it, he wanted to teach the

kids a lesson they wouldn't forget. He called a policeman friend and asked him to come out and scare them into realizing the seriousness of what they had done. Al, being the youngest, cried when the policeman showed up at the house because not only was he scared but he thought his older brother Dennis was going to go to jail. Because no one was hurt, however, they were all just given a strong warning to never throw stones at trucks again. Al remembers the feeling of relief that he felt when the policeman left. They all vowed to never do that again. It was a lesson learned for the Fredette boys.

Having been discouraged from playing by the highway in front of the house, the boys turned their imaginations toward the seemingly endless woods behind it. One day they decided to start the Smokey the Bear Club. All the Fredette boys were members of the club, and a friend or two could join if they voted to let them in. It was Al's job to climb a high pine tree to be the lookout for forest fires.

They all thought that since Al was the lookout person, there ought to be some smoke once in a while so he could do his job. The boys started a little fire to create some smoke for Al to see. This dubious idea played out as you might expect: the small fire very quickly turned into a bigger fire, and before the Fredette boys' Smokey the Bear Club knew it, the fire department had to come to put it out. Al doesn't remember who called the fire department—probably one of the neighbors—but he does remember all the boys circling around through the woods and out to the front of the house, where their parents stood watching the fire trucks and firefighters putting out the grass fire. The boys innocently asked what was going on and managed to divert attention away from themselves as the culprits. The Smokey the Bear Club was scratched off their list of things to do.

In their less mischievous moments, the Fredette boys played sports every day. They played baseball and football and soccer when the weather was good, and in the winter they played ice hockey at the rink in Comstock, near the prison. They used to make their younger sister Bonnie be the full-time goalie, whether she liked it or not, and it turned out she held her own in sports with all of her brothers. She could hit in baseball and she could catch, much to their surprise and delight. Al also prided himself on being able to catch any football thrown near him or baseball hit near him.

As the Fredette siblings got older, they used to play football in the backyard—regularly playing after dark with the help of the dim lighting Craig rigged up. The backyard night games were halted when Al and his nephew, Mark, collided, and both wound up in the emergency room to get stitches in their foreheads. After that the boys decided to take their football to the front yard, where there was more light from the front porch, and named that Fredette Field.

Fredette Field was the setting of many enjoyable hours of football. Al and Kay were dating at the time, and Kay fondly remembers the coed games they played there.

Typical of a Taft, Kay was known for her quickness and broken-field running, and Bonnie Fredette was a good target for the quarterback because she was tall and could catch the ball if it was thrown to her. Those games, good memories for both Kay and Al, fed their competitive spirits.

Al was the youngest of the boys but was not pampered or babied by the older siblings, so he developed a real mental and physical toughness. As the youngest of four boys and as rambunctious as they were, he had no choice but to play injured at times. It was a matter of survival in some cases. Al remembers being beaten up many times and getting knocked out a couple of times in the process, but he never shied away. Those acquired attributes, coupled with his inborn desire to compete and win, are some of the ingredients that go into making a good athlete. Al and Kay's kids were the recipients of good qualities and athletic genes from both sides of the family.

Al's love of sports carried into his high school years, and he became a four-sport letterman in baseball, football, basketball, and track at Whitehall High. He earned a letter sweater, which had an emblem sewed on the pocket and was considered quite a high honor in sports.

His events in track were the half mile and the triple jump, and he held the school record for the triple jump for a few years. Baseball was a sport that he really excelled at, and at one time he even contemplated trying out for the pros. He was a center fielder and could catch anything that was hit even remotely near him. Even now there are times when someone misses a difficult catch on TV and Al will say, "I could have caught that." He was never at a loss for confidence in his sports abilities.

Al still plays basketball with his brother Dennis, and they have the same desire to win that they have always had—even if the physical skills are no longer the same. Al was not known for his offense, but his defense was relentless. That was the hallmark of his intense competitive nature.

In college, Al was a walk-on on the football team at Central Connecticut State and became a starting safety. But the position was very short-lived because an injury he sustained during the first game—torn ligaments in his knee—meant he had to wear a cast for six weeks. As it turned out, Al was able to go to Central Connecticut for only a year because of financial constraints. His parents were moving to Arizona at that time because of his mother's health, and they weren't able to help him. His mother was heartbroken to have to leave their home, but they had to do what was best for her health. So, after a year in Connecticut, Al had to quit school and go to work in hopes of returning in the future.

Al eventually returned to school, but it wasn't in Connecticut. Following his adopted Mormon faith, he applied at BYU and was accepted. By then he was married to Kay, and they both went out to Utah so he could follow his plan of becoming an attorney. Once again, finances contributed to changes in his plans. He had attended BYU for a semester when he was offered a good job back home. He and Kay went back to Glens Falls to raise their family. Al eventually became a financial advisor, and Kay obtained a teaching degree, but she preferred being a substitute teacher for many years because of the flexibility it gave her to be with her family.

Kay's and Al's parenting skills were challenged to the utmost when T. J. was an adolescent. By then, he had begun what has become a lifetime fight with anxiety, though he has since learned many ways of coping with this affliction.

Jimmer also understood from a young age what it was like to struggle, mentally and emotionally as he watched his brother.

CHAPTER FIVE

FEAR

For as long as an hour, Al Fredette would circle Glens Falls Middle School. Next to him in the car, his oldest son was an anxiety-ridden wreck.

"You have to go to school," Al would tell T. J., over and over.

Sometimes he said it gently. Sometimes he said it sternly. Sometimes it worked. Sometimes it didn't. And even when it did work, T. J. routinely would enter the building and head straight to the boys' bathroom, hiding himself in a stall. Or he would end up sitting in the nurse's office, feigning illness in hopes of being sent home.

The panic attacks he began having at age 11 were getting worse. There was some history of it on both sides of the family, and panic disorder has been known to run in families. But T. J.'s situation was unusually severe and debilitating.

FEAR

According to the American Academy of Child & Adolescent Psychiatry, more than 3 million Americans will experience panic disorder in their lifetime. Many will be afflicted with it as children. T. J. was one of those—but it was only the beginning of the mental issues that would burden and challenge him throughout his growth from adolescence to adulthood.

At first, T. J. was able to hide the attacks from his parents and his siblings—he would put on his customary carefree face whenever he was around them at home. The "master of disguise," as he called himself, never let on how much he struggled with simply going to school like every other kid.

Inside, he was embarrassed by what was happening—by the strange weakness in his legs that accompanied every step toward the school building, by the irresistible compulsion to avoid his friends and classmates and teachers, by the overwhelming desire to bolt from his desk when class began. But he kept those feelings under wraps as long as possible.

"Nobody knew anything was wrong with me," T. J. said. "But there was. Something was extremely wrong."

By eighth grade, the anxiety could not be hidden any longer. Grades and composure slipping, T. J. had to admit what was going on. He was constantly panicked, and the attacks were crippling.

When T. J. went to bed in the small upstairs room he shared with Jimmer, he frequently had nightmares. Just as frequently he woke up frozen by anxiety, dreading the coming of the day. Watching the darkness inevitably give way to light in the bedroom brought the horrible realization that he was about to encounter a cycle of fear yet again.

"I would wake up really early, sweaty and just scared," T. J. said. "As soon as I saw that light coming through the window, I knew another day was starting, and right away I'd get these panic attacks and not be able to go back to sleep. I was petrified to go to school. I'd resist my parents' efforts to get me out the door to go to school."

During eighth grade, T. J. estimates he missed 40 to 50 days of school—very few of them for any visible physical ailment. He missed so much class time that he barely made it to ninth grade. In fact, to pass eighth grade, he had to consult with his teachers and do make-up work during the summer. Fortunately for T. J., the school did not let him slip through the cracks, and neither did his parents, but the process of recovering academically was difficult—and the emotional impact of his struggles was significant.

The outgoing third-grader who cajoled his principal into letting him do an Elvis impersonation for the entire school became a stressed-out eighth grader who loathed even walking into the building. At a socially and emotionally vulnerable age, T. J. felt as though he was failing himself and his family, and nobody could understand why.

FEAR

As an adult lyricist, he wrote about how those child-hood panic attacks affected him:

Eleven years old
Life seemed so rough
All the counseling in the world
Couldn't be enough
Tears in my eyes
Staring at the wall
Locked in a stall
Too scared just to walk the hall
And not scared of a bully
No, not at all
I was scared of my brain
I was being mauled
By these panic attacks
It's like I can't breathe
How many times can I get the teacher to believe
That I gotta see the nurse
That I gotta leave
Faking sick was the greatest skill I achieved
I'm too young to be dealing with this
How's it possible for me to be feeling like this?
I was given good friends
Good family life
Good home
Good health
So why must I fight through the darkness

When everything around me is light
My nightmares had me scared to go to sleep at
  night
Every morning I was too scared to see the light
A blanket over my eyes
Trying to block my sight
The sunlight meant another day I had to suffer
I was drowning in my thoughts
I was going under
Too depressed to understand being happy
Being buried alive
I could see the devil laughing at me
No weapons to fight back
I live scared
God sent me to earth way too unprepared
And unaware of the army that was facing me
Too slow for the enemy that was chasing me
I lost faith so my family had to pray for me

T. J.'s parents spent years praying for him and worrying about him. Academics were always a struggle for Al and Kay's middle child, even before the panic attacks began. In fact, Jimmer's earliest memory of T. J. was a family celebration over a rare scholastic success his brother enjoyed.

"I remember one time he did really, really well on one of his tests," Jimmer recalled. "He was so excited about it, and my parents were so excited about it—he didn't do well in school—but because he was excited, I got excited.

It didn't happen too often, that's why I remember it. T. J. was high-spirited and was constantly struggling with his anxieties so school was always a challenge for him."

This development was a jarring departure from the jaunty neighborhood pied piper, the one who organized the games and doled out the nicknames and made sure everyone was having fun all the time. He could still be that way at home, but that attitude disappeared at school where he was constantly worrying and enduring simmering stress.

Jimmer and Lindsay were generally unaware of what was going on with T. J. They were young, and their parents, as much as possible, shielded them from the reality of their brother's struggles. What would it help for them to know? With Jimmer in elementary school and Lindsay in high school, they weren't around middle-schooler T. J. enough to know how much class time he was missing or why.

"We had different schedules a lot of the time," Lindsay said. "I would go to school earlier, and then our dad would drop T. J. off. So, a lot of times, I wouldn't know that he hadn't been at school until later. When he first started having the problems, we weren't aware of the depth of what was going on. I mean, T. J. and I were really close throughout our growing up because we were just two years apart. We were best friends. We were one of those lucky brother-and-sister companionships that never fought. We just always played together all the time. We had a group of friends we ran around with in the neighborhood. And he was always such a happy, athletic, active kid. Always going and going and going. We made up all these games together that we would play. So in junior high and high school, there was definitely a change—not in our closeness, but you could tell that his demeanor had changed. He just wasn't that same worry-free, carefree kid."

After barely getting through eighth grade, T. J. regrouped and did better in ninth and tenth grades. Then the panic issues returned his junior year at Glens Falls High School, coinciding with Lindsay's leaving for college at BYU. The separation from his childhood best friend weighed heavily on him.

The timing of his illness was especially bad for his athletic career, since T. J. was playing varsity football and basketball. This was his long-awaited chance to play in front of real crowds—perhaps even in front of college recruiters—but that dream was compromised by his anxiety. Even when he had succeeded in enduring the day at school, panic attacks would sometimes set in on bus rides to away games. His practice time and playing time suffered because his school attendance suffered. He again missed roughly 50 days of school and had to scramble academically to advance to his senior year.

Al and Kay, known for their generosity toward all their children's friends, had to turn their compassion inward. They invested a lot of time and money in trying to find out what was wrong with T. J., working with school counselors and medical professionals.

"I was going through depression, taking all these medications, going to doctors," T. J. said. "I was just miserable all the time." He wrote:

> *My emotions controlling my whole entire day*
> *Feeling pain but there's no way that I could say*
> *How I'm feeling dismay*
> *Of why I'm feeling this way*
> *There's nothing for me to explain*
> *This is the game that I play*
> *And I play it every day*

T. J. rallied again as a senior, feeling better most of the year. He went to class, he played sports, and he enjoyed an important year in every young adult's life. But going away to college the way Lindsay had was out of the question for him. His grades were iffy, and his emotional state was fragile enough that options were limited.

Instead of heading off to Brigham Young University or any other four-year school, T. J. enrolled at Adirondack Community College in Queensbury, the town adjoining Glens Falls. He was the starting point guard for the Timberwolves, distributing the ball and making friends with his new teammates. The school that came with playing basketball was viewed as a necessary evil.

Jimmer went to watch many of the rough-and-tumble junior college games, which were played in front of crowds that were usually smaller than those at Glens Falls High. The games were often, as Al recalled, "heated and loquacious and pugnacious." That suited T. J., who was never one to back away from a challenge or confrontation.

The teams T. J. competed for and against were made up of talented players, many of whom had been culled from New York City and whose talents had been overlooked or who had gotten into trouble and been bypassed by bigger, four-year programs. By the second semester the roster always dwindled due to academic problems or players quitting—that was the nature of the junior-college beast. But not T. J., who was happy simply to be playing.

"I enjoyed the basketball," he said. "It was probably one of the best junior college leagues in the country, and we had a competitive team. I liked my teammates."

Some of those teammates ended up hanging out in the basement of the house on Odgen Street. That was part of the deal with T. J.—everyone he knew was welcome to be part of the Fredette family. What had been true in junior high and high school remained true in college.

It was good to be on a team, and it was good to be home. But the schoolwork remained a struggle. Other than creative writing, T. J. didn't enjoy his academics any more in junior college than he had while growing up.

"I didn't know what I wanted to do, so I was taking liberal arts classes where I did well enough to be eligible to play ball," he said. "It was pretty much the easiest major. It was different from high school—having that freedom where it's up to you to be on time or go to class or turn in your work, I didn't handle that too well."

That freedom brought back some of the old anxiety issues, but by then T. J. had devised several coping mechanisms to deal with them. Where he once had been a master of disguise, he had gotten assistance in slowly becoming a master of mind control in an effort to simply make do on a daily basis.

"I told myself, 'I can't let this ruin my life. I'm going to learn to fight through it,'" he said.

Fighting through the panic required using methods that T. J. had started working on back in eighth grade, when it became clear that constantly feigning illness was not going to work. When there was no escape from his desk, he had three methods of coping:

1. *Transporting himself into the future.*

When class was fraying his nerves, T. J. would think beyond the school day—what was coming up that he would enjoy? Maybe it was basketball practice or a game. Maybe it was a movie or a show that would be on TV that night. He took himself there as best he could.

"I could almost envision watching that movie or making that play in a game," he said. "I'd play the game in my head. Those good vibes helped me fight off the anxiety attacks."

2. *Transporting himself into the past.*

If there wasn't anything on T. J.'s to-do list that was easy to look forward to, the alternative was to dial in to recent history. Maybe it was winning a big game, making a key play, or achieving a rare academic success. Whatever it was, tapping into the positive feeling that came with that pleasant experience helped.

"I tried to relive those moments," T. J. said. "I said to myself, 'I know I'm struggling now, but I'm going to have that good feeling again sometime soon.' I really tried to remember how that felt. Thinking about some past success helped get the serotonin level up in my brain again."

3. Embracing his inner competitor.

This involved simply getting into a mind-set such as he would need in preparing for a challenging basketball game—and envisioning victory.

"It was like when you play basketball and you say, 'There is no way I'm going to let this guy beat me.' I knew how to compete in a game, and I decided to bring that same attitude and effort to my struggle against the anxiety attacks. I basically said to myself: 'I don't care how bad it gets. I don't care if I die in this chair. I'm not going to leave this classroom. I am not going to give in.' I just tried to will myself through it."

One small victory at a time, T. J. had arduously climbed the academic ladder until he graduated from junior high, then high school, and then community college. He'd gotten to play basketball at every level on the way—but maxing out at Adirondack C. C. and moving on to an adult men's rec league had not been his childhood hoop dream.

It had become clear well before then that he was never going to be a college star and play on TV. He was never going to play in the pros and make an unimaginable living.

But if T. J. couldn't do those things, it only deepened his resolve that one day Jimmer would.

CHAPTER SIX

TRUST

One sweltering summer day, Kay Fredette came home and encountered what she considered to be a disturbing scene in the backyard: Seven-year-old Jimmer was dribbling the ball in work gloves while T. J. knocked him around. Jimmer's cherubic face was dirt-streaked, and his hair was curling as it always does when he sweats profusely. He wasn't complaining, but he didn't look comfortable.

The gloves and the shoves were 14-year-old T. J.'s brainstorming methods to improve Jimmer's ball handling—if the little guy could dribble under those conditions, it would be easy in a gym playing with bare hands and officials who would call fouls.

Kay thought that was excessive. T. J. shrugged.

"He's got water," T. J. said, as if any other creature

comforts would be akin to a spa treatment instead of a serious practice session.

Jimmer didn't mind it. If he hadn't liked it, he wouldn't have done it. Since Jimmer had been old enough to bounce a ball, T. J. had been coaching him. Dealing with his own issues at school, in basketball, and in general were draining and difficult. Helping Jimmer become a basketball player was not. T. J.'s mind always seemed more at ease when the subject was someone else—especially someone in the family.

"It's funny," said T. J.'s sister, Lindsay. "For all the struggles and things that he's been through and issues that he deals with in his own head, he is always able to look out and see what other people need. He's always helping people, and he is a *magnet* for people."

He was a basketball magnet for Jimmer, seven years younger but always ready to go where big brother went and do what big brother did.

Al Fredette taught both his sons—and many of their teammates—the fundamentals of basketball while they were growing up. He played with and against them in parks, in gyms, and in the cultural hall at the LDS church. He helped organize Amateur Athletic Union (AAU) teams, coached them, traveled with them. He took the Fredette boys and their friends to play in 3-on-3 tournaments all over the Northeast, serving as an unofficial coach. And he dispensed plenty of postgame critiques—the good and the bad—to his boys and their friends while driving home from those events.

But that was more organized stuff. T. J. was Jimmer's unofficial coach, the backyard improviser, the guy who would suddenly dream up something on a summer day and have Jimmer try it out. He loved devising all kinds of off-the-wall drills to improve his little brother's game.

This was T. J.'s fertile, restless mind at work. He's never been a sound sleeper—something the family attributes to a brain that just doesn't shut down. His penchant for creativity led him to dream up nicknames for everyone in the family and most of their friends. He organized the backyard tournaments, complete with awards. He did the Elvis thing. When he started rapping, he came up with albums entitled *Albert Rhymestein* and *The Showman Empire,* the latter featuring T. J. dressed in Roman garb.

And for a long time, one of the primary outlets for T. J.'s energy and imagination was Jimmer and the neighborhood kids. Specifically, their progress as basketball players.

T. J. enjoyed putting on those backyard tournaments for the young kids in the neighborhood and handing out his trophies as awards. Naturally, the kids reciprocated that interest—they loved being around T. J. and winning his contests.

T. J. especially got a kick out of his so-called "Hustle Award," which basically meant that every time a ball went over the fence into a neighbor's yard—which was often— somebody had to go retrieve it. And that somebody was not going to be T. J. or his older friends. So as the ball would clear the fence, T. J. would wink at his buddies and yell, "Hustle Award!" and the little guys would scurry to get it while the older guys laughed.

But what he enjoyed most was working with Jimmer. The idea of helping shape a future star appealed to T. J. He'd helped Glens Falls High make its first-ever appearance in the state tournament, but T. J. knew his own career had its limitations—he wasn't as big as Jimmer, didn't have his shooting stroke, and had the anxiety issues to deal with. So he concentrated his energies on the brother who would follow him and eclipse him as a player.

Reflecting on the successes Jimmer has enjoyed, the boys' uncle Lee Taft said: "Even in high school, T. J. lived through Jimmer, T. J. knew Jimmer had something special. He saw something special there and worked with him.

"He could have very easily said, 'Jimmer, get lost. I want to play with my friends.' He didn't do that. He saw the potential for this moment we're in now and did what he could to help make it happen."

So that creative mind went to work, dreaming and scheming unique ways to make Jimmer the best possible player.

"He was always coming up with stuff," Jimmer said. "Maybe it was a better drill, and maybe it wasn't. But it made it fun, so I wanted to keep playing. I wanted to play all the time because it was fun to do that type of stuff.

His mind was always working and trying to create new things."

Among T. J.'s more memorable stratagems was the Church Hallway Dribbling Drill, which was performed at the LDS church in Glens Falls. Instead of having Jimmer do generic dribbling drills on a court, working on moves while keeping his eyes up and not looking at the ball, T. J. came up with his own variation.

T. J. knew that kids from places like Glens Falls would be doubted when they went to the city gyms in Albany and New York City and Hartford. He knew they wouldn't get the benefit of the doubt from college recruiters. He knew that fundamentals and execution and skill set had to be augmented with a toughness you couldn't find at the city park.

But it could be found in prison. So that's where Jimmer and T. J. went.

The Fredettes' next-door neighbor on Ogden Street had a relative who ran recreation programs at two nearby medium-security prisons: Mount McGregor Correctional Facility in Wilton, and Washington Correctional Facility in Comstock. The family member knew T. J. was a basketball player, and in 2007 the prison administrators were working on a plan to reward inmates for good behavior by letting them play basketball against a team of guys from the outside.

The question was put to T. J.: "How would you like to organize the team to play against the prisoners?"

Law-abiding citizens vs. convicts. In front of a crowd of fellow cons. And prison guards standing by. T. J. was, of course, all in.

"I would love to do that," he said.

The Fredettes were always up for a game of hoops—but T. J. knew this was a potential learning opportunity for his younger brother. He was immediately envisioning a toughening experience that was beyond anything to be found in Glens Falls.

This was a couple of months after he had Jimmer sign The Contract, so T. J. was focused on the future. This was another step in making the aim of The Contract a reality.

"He was just thinking ahead," Jimmer said. "He thought, 'Wow, this would be cool. It would be a great story.' He was thinking about all of that type of stuff before we even went into it. I could tell he was really excited about it."

Jimmer's response: "It's just another adventure with T. J., I guess."

At first, Jimmer thought T. J. was taking him to Great Meadow—a maximum-security correctional facility that's across the street from the Washington facility. Jimmer balked at the thought of playing against convicted murderers. Assured that they were "only" going to a medium-security prison, Jimmer was fine with that.

Al Fredette was fine with it as well. Kay Fredette, not so much.

"We talked her into it," Jimmer said. "We could always

talk her into things. It's always a 'No!' the first time you want to do something—every time, 'No!' And then we'd say, 'Come on, Mom!' Then you talk her into it, and she'd finally say, 'Oh, all right . . .'"

After filling out a small mountain of paperwork for each player, the dates of the games were set. Upon arrival at the penitentiary, Jimmer, T. J., and their teammates had to sign in and walk through the labyrinth of gates and bars. The deeper they got into the facility, the more palpable the feeling became of what it's like to leave your freedom behind.

"They open the gates, and then they close them right behind you and lock them," Jimmer said.

Eventually the boys passed through the prison yard, the high fence with razor wire coiled at the top and the inmates milling around. Having seen more than a few movies, mingling with real-life criminals in a real-life correctional facility made for a fairly unnerving pregame initiation into a different world.

"They're walking right past you and stuff," Jimmer said. "They're kind of thinking, 'What are you guys doing here?' They don't know what's going on at first. And then you walk into the gym."

Jimmer was pleasantly surprised by the courts—fairly roomy and in decent condition. One of them even had an NBA-length three-point line painted on it. The bleachers would always be empty at first, but security guards were posted in all four corners of the gym. There were other guards watching from the windows and by the bleachers.

"There were two doors, one on each end of the bleachers, and then all of a sudden they opened them and the inmates just started walking in and filling up the seats," Jimmer recalled. "And they'd fill the place every time because they loved watching it. And they'd bet everything on it. They'd bet cigarettes and whatever they had on them.

"Most of them would bet that the inmates would win. But there were always a few who would be on our side. They said some crazy things. You could hear tons and tons of different comments. And you saw some crazy things. Just being in prison—well, it's prison. So, you would play. It was intimidating at first because they were yelling at you and most of them didn't want you to win. And you would always have one ref that was from the outside and one ref who was an inmate. They would keep it that way."

The officials never had to worry about an altercation, and the guards never had to control the crowd. There were some good players, some not as good, and the prisoners played hard but clean. If an inmate fouled an outsider hard, knocking him to the ground, he helped him up. Once the games began, it was pretty much normal basketball—being played in a surreal setting.

"You just started playing and having a good time and being competitive like always," Jimmer said. "We weren't intimidated or anything like that. None of our guys were scared. We just wanted to go out there and play and have a good time. And nothing ever happened. There were never any altercations because the inmates knew if they did do anything, the officials would take this privilege away. And they didn't want that. They wanted to keep it going, and they had a good time playing."

By the time he began participating in the prison games, Jimmer had already made a name for himself on the outside. He was a senior star at Glens Falls High and headed to BYU, so the prisoners knew something about him. He scored 40 points against the prisoners on that first visit and never had fewer than 30 points in the games he played there. His teams never lost a game.

Combining his talent with good sportsmanship, respect for the inmates, and the very fact that he was willing to go play there, it didn't take long before Jimmer had a new and novel fan base. As his prowess and fame grew, so did the pride the prisoners took in him—those who got to play against him or to see him play, up close and personal.

"They would follow my career," Jimmer said, "and every time T. J. went back and I wasn't there, they would always ask about me—the inmates and the guards. They were always asking, 'How's Jimmer doing?' Stuff like that. So, that was kind of cool."

Over the next few years, some of Jimmer's most loyal fans were behind bars. The TV lounges in the Mount McGregor dorm areas were tuned to BYU games whenever they were on, and attendance to watch the games was high. Newspaper clippings about Jimmer's BYU career were posted in the joint, and inmates who were around the longest started passing down an oral history of the times when Jimmer came to play ball right there among the prisoners.

"It was a really fun experience," Jimmer said. "Very intimidating at first. I don't think it really helped me much basketball-wise. But it definitely helped my mental toughness—just being able to block things out. They say the worst things you can possibly hear, and no outside fan can top that, no matter how hostile the setting. In the prison, the gyms are small and the spectators are right on top of you, and it's so intimate that you can hear everything. So, it was an interesting, fun experience—something that not many people get to do."

To be sure, the language heard in the prison gyms was not replicated in the Marriott Center, BYU's home court. It wasn't even replicated at the toughest gyms in the Mountain West Conference—The Pit at New Mexico, the Thomas & Mack Center at UNLV, the Huntsman Center at Utah, or Viejas Arena at San Diego State. No wonder Jimmer handled road games well while at BYU. What could compare to playing road games in prison?

"Some of those places, some of the fans are crazy, and they say stuff," Jimmer said. "But in prison they'd say whatever they wanted. *Tons* of foul language. Anything that you can think of, they said it. They were just trying to get into your head, trying to win a bet. But a lot of times, the inmates would see we were pretty good, and there was often a change in betting. All of a sudden, they started to want the outsiders to win, and they would change sides, and we would get more cheers as the game went on."

That was exactly what T. J. wanted Jimmer to get out of the prison-ball experience: an increased toughness and the ability to focus in difficult surroundings. What Jimmer learned inside the razor wire came with him into the real world, especially in college.

"Some players will fold if people are all over them," T. J. said. "Jimmer feeds off the opposition and just gets better and better."

The game that most exemplified that was at UNLV during Jimmer's senior year. Jimmer was taunted pregame by the Runnin' Rebels fans, and they were pouring it on the BYU star as UNLV raced to a 10-point lead late in the first half. It looked as though Jimmer would finish his four-year college career without having beaten the Rebels in Las Vegas.

T. J. was watching on TV back in New York with a friend. He heard the gym roaring and sensed that Jimmer was ready to take over.

"I could see Jimmer's face on TV, and I said to my friend, 'Watch what happens now,'" T. J. recalled. "Coming down court on fast break, Jimmer just pulled up and hit a three, and it was like, 'All right, here we go.' Then he just kept hitting threes. The BYU bench was going nuts, and you could see on the UNLV guys' faces, it was like,

'Uh-oh, we turned him on.' It was probably one of my proudest moments, watching that game."

Jimmer personally erased that 10-point deficit by swishing four 3-point shots in a four-minute span, the last of which gave BYU the lead for good. He finished the game with 39 points and one of the sweetest victories of his college career.

That response when the gym was all over him? That was a prison-ball lesson come to life. That's why T. J. took him into medium security to begin with. To promote toughness in the face of adversity, in front of a hostile crowd, without losing your cool.

Keeping his cool was harder for T. J. He had to adjust his personality to play in the prison games. His famously quick, on-court temper had to be kept in check. That was no place for the trash talk and altercations of Crandall Park. Not with these guys—and frankly, the inmates didn't want that, either.

Jimmer never questioned the choice of venue or opponent. He would follow T. J. anywhere. Even to prison.

As Jimmer's game developed, he outstripped his need for familial coaching. But that didn't mean T. J. stepped into the background. He evolved from drill instructor to more of a motivational consultant.

They talked before every game—sometimes in person, sometimes on the phone, sometimes via text. T. J. would relate a movie scene or character to the upcoming game (Joe Pesci was a frequent subject). Or he would text a joke about the opponent's mascot. There was always a fresh play on words from big brother to little brother on game day—something to make Jimmer laugh and then help him focus.

"If it's a really big game, I'd have to call," T. J. said. "I know he knows how important it is—he's got it anyway—but I want to reinforce it. I want to hear how he sounds, hear his voice, and find out where his head is. And I want him to know we're excited."

Throughout every step of his basketball journey, Jimmer has never lacked enthusiastic family support. But T. J., more than anyone else, was the Fredette with vision for Jimmer. He could see his future unfolding and devised every crazy method he could think of to make it a reality.

Said Jimmer: "He's never led me astray."

But even if T. J. believed in Jimmer and Jimmer believed in himself, they had to convince the world outside of 26 Ogden Street just how good a basketball player the kid could become. And that would not be easy.

CHAPTER SEVEN

DOUBT

From the look of it, the Glens Falls Civic Center wouldn't inspire much in the way of sporting romance. It is a big, square, multipurpose brick building that opened in 1979 and sits inartistically along the Hudson River in an otherwise quaint and charming downtown.

Primarily it is known as the home of the Adirondack Phantoms, a minor-league hockey franchise that has enjoyed a fair amount of success if you judge by the banners hanging from the rafters. But in March the Civic Center also hosts the New York public high school state basketball tournament. For one week every year, young Jimmer Fredette found the 4,806-seat building to be a basketball cathedral. To him, it was every bit as dreamy a place as Cameron Indoor Stadium, the Dean Smith Center, or Hinkle Fieldhouse.

When Jimmer was in elementary school and junior

high, Al Fredette would often take him to the Civic Center with a ticket to the tournament and $5 in his pocket. Jimmer would stay all day watching games—the morning session, the afternoon session, the evening session. If they were playing, Jimmer the basketball junkie was watching. He was in heaven.

"I'd watch every game," he recalled. "I loved it. I'd sit there by myself most of the time. My dad would come sometimes if he could. Every once in a while, a friend would come—but they couldn't sit there and watch it that long. But I'd watch every game, and I just loved it.

"I tried to get the players' autographs. It didn't matter who. It didn't matter if the kid was awful or not. And I'd go up to them, and they'd be flattered, 'cause they would think, 'You want *my* autograph?' And I would say, 'Yeah.'"

Throughout the bitter winter months in upstate New York, Jimmer watched basketball on TV every chance he got—pro games, college games, whatever was on. And of course he went to see T. J. play for Glens Falls High. But the state tournament was special—a private opportunity in his hometown to go to the Civic Center and see his dream play out in front of him.

Before Jimmer could become an NBA draft pick or a college Player of the Year, he wanted to become a high school star. He wanted to play in the state tournament like the boys he spent all day watching every March.

"I used to envision myself out there," Jimmer said.

"And imagine the crowd packed and it being crazy—and us winning."

That day would come, of course, the day when Jimmer would be the one playing in the state tournament and signing autographs and transfixing young boys.

To the delight of upstate New York, he carried the hometown team to the Class A state title game his senior season. They lost, but it was a landmark achievement for his town. He scored more than 2,400 points at Glens Falls High, sixth-most in New York state history.

The kid whose shooting altered the way backyard pickup games were played at the Fredette house never stopped. The kid whose shooting tickled halftime crowds at Glens Falls when he was a youngster kept swishing shots right through high school. The promise his dad and brother saw so vividly—and nurtured so enthusiastically—was being fulfilled right in front of them.

As a freshman, Jimmer scored 32 points in a sectional playoff game. As a sophomore, he guided Glens Falls into the sectional finals, but encountered a rare failure at that point.

With less than a second to play against Burnt Hills High School, Jimmer stepped to the foul line. Glens Falls trailed by a point. He was shooting two free throws.

He missed them both. The season was over.

"I felt awful," Jimmer said. "I'd failed my team. I could have won the game easily. After that I made 100 free throws after every workout. I was never going to do that again. I still do it to this day."

In college, Jimmer became one of the most accurate foul shooters in the nation, making at least 85 percent of his free throws each season at Brigham Young. It's in his makeup to turn failure into fertilizer for future growth. He's made a career out of it.

Starting early in high school, Jimmer would issue himself challenges while working out alone—if you want to bring fans to their feet, you have to become a great player. If you want other young boys to one day come to the state tournament and ask for *your* autograph, you have to perfect your game. Right here, right now, this very workout.

"That's what I'd think about—I'd want everybody in the crowd to be watching *me* and to be thinking about *me* and to be like, 'Wow! He's a good player,'" Jimmer said. "I'd try to get that in my head. And if I don't make this shot right here, then I'm not going to get any better, and so they're not going to be impressed. And that was my mind-set. So, I have to go out there and do a drill until I do it correctly and I make it 100 percent. And if I don't make it, then I have to keep doing it until I do.

"I've practiced that way for a long time because I thought about that *all* the way through high school— even my freshman year. I thought about that and I wanted everybody to be impressed—all my friends to be impressed, all the girls to be impressed. I wanted everybody to think, 'Wow, Jimmer's *it*. He's the guy.' I used that as fuel to motivate myself. That was my mind-set."

But even as his notoriety spread in upstate New York, there was only so much he could do to erase the doubts of recruiters. Despite all the successes, there was one day that never came—the day a famous coach from a big-time college came to Glens Falls and offered Jimmer a scholarship to play for him. He was a North Carolina fan as a kid, but North Carolina never called. He was a Syracuse fan by proximity, but the school was never serious about giving him a full ride. There were Big East schools within a few hours' drive in all directions, but they never paid much attention.

"I just kind of brushed it all off," Jimmer said. "I just said, 'These are the guys that are coming after me.' And I knew I was better than the kids that they were getting and I could play with those kids or whatever. But there's just nothing you can do about it. And there's no sense in sulking about it. You just go out there and make the best of it."

While Jimmer shrugged off the recruiting snubs and kept playing, his family was frustrated and puzzled. T. J. said all the right things to his little brother—about how NBA scouts can find great players anywhere, not just at the power programs—but wasn't sure he fully believed it himself.

Jimmer excelled in summer AAU and shoe-company tournaments and camps in front of bleachers filled with prominent coaches, but that never translated into endless phone calls or a torrent of personal mail from those coaches. His AAU coach with the Albany City Rocks, Tim Moseman, called him "the best-kept secret in basketball." The secret somehow never got out.

There were form letters and other group mailings that went to dozens of other recruits. But there weren't a lot of the handwritten notes that big-time coaches send to the players they want the most.

"I don't understand it, because these coaches were right there watching," T. J. said. "Jimmer was Co-MVP of Rumble in the Bronx [a major AAU tournament] and did great at national tournaments when future NBA lottery picks O. J. Mayo and Michael Beasley were there.

"I guess it was because they had certain players on their radar already. But it was right in front of their eyes."

The coaches' brains didn't believe what their eyes were telling them. They didn't believe that a white guard from a small town could score in college the same way he was scoring in high school and in AAU ball. They believed the higher level of competition would expose him. They were sure quicker guards would devour him.

"They thought I wasn't athletic enough," Jimmer said. "They thought I couldn't get my shot off in college. I had many people tell me that.

"I would think, 'Are you kidding me? It has nothing to do with that—you just get a little bit of space and shoot it and make it. I mean, as long as they don't block my shot, it's going to go in. They're not going to block my shot every time, so I'm going to make shots. I'm going to show you.' And that's the way you've got to think."

The recruiters didn't know what a master of the half-inch Jimmer had become in those training sessions with Uncle Lee. They didn't appreciate how he could gain an advantage in tight quarters, contort his body to get a shooting angle, or make plays with either hand. They didn't grasp Jimmer's indefinable, innate feel for how to score—for sizing up a defender and knowing what would work and how to get it done.

The recruiters saw a stereotype that usually doesn't work at the highest level of college ball and failed to see past that stereotype.

"It's something that I learned when I was really young—how to create enough space to get the shot off," Jimmer said. "Because there are definitely more athletic and quicker guys out there who are very big and long. But to me it didn't matter. Getting your shot off is about understanding how to get enough space to avoid getting your shot blocked or altered. If you can get that little bit of space, you can shoot it. And you have to have the confidence that it's going to go in. I think it's a gift that you have. It's not something you can work on necessarily all that much. It's more of a sense thing. A gift. I was very blessed in that category."

With so many basketball coaches unmoved by his game, the most attention Jimmer got for a while from recruiters was as a football prospect. He was New York's all-state wide receiver as a junior in high school, and perennial power Penn State came to Glens Falls to scout him. Boston College and Notre Dame also showed interest.

With his size and skills, Jimmer was an intriguing prospect. T. J. had played receiver before him, but at that time Glens Falls rarely threw the ball. By the time Jimmer got to high school the no-huddle, spread-offense craze had arrived, and he got plenty of passes thrown in his direction.

But Jimmer's heart was in basketball. He stopped playing football before his senior year.

"I liked playing football games," Jimmer said. "I hated football practice. It was my least favorite thing. The games were a lot of fun. I played both ways—offense and defense—receiver and outside linebacker. It was really fun to play in front of everybody and score a touchdown. I liked baseball too, but it was also a little too slow for me."

Still, the premier basketball programs never joined the chase. Jimmer did get some attention from Syracuse assistant Mike Hopkins, but the school never bothered to invite him on an official visit—one that's paid for by the school and where the coaches roll out the red carpet for the recruits they really want. The best the Fredettes could get from Syracuse was an unofficial visit to watch practice—expenses paid for out of their own pocket—and head coach Jim Boeheim wasn't overly enthusiastic.

At least the Syracuse Orange had a reasonable excuse for their lukewarm interest in Jimmer: point guard Jonny Flynn of nearby Niagara Falls had committed to Syracuse before his high school junior year had started. Flynn was a much more heralded recruit than Jimmer.

So despite his high school accolades and AAU successes, Jimmer became a second-tier prospect. Marshall and Massachusetts offered scholarships. Nearby Siena was dying to get him, and Jimmer was interested. Under Coach Fran McCaffrey the Saints played an up-tempo style that seemed well-suited to his game.

But then, after his sophomore year, Jimmer decided to attend a summer basketball camp at Lindsay Fredette's alma mater, BYU. That camp changed everything.

"He just tore it up," T. J. said. "He just killed everybody."

Suddenly, Siena had formidable competition for the obscure point guard from just up the Interstate. The Cougars coaching staff recognized Jimmer's talents, latched on to him, and never let go. BYU Assistant Coach John Wardenburg watched almost his every dribble at that camp and had company from his boss.

"I was able to watch him play five or six hours the first day," BYU head coach Dave Rose said of that fateful camp. "Then all day the next day. And all day the day after that."

Rose saw a guy with big feet and an occasionally awkward way of shooting the ball. But he also saw a player with a limitless repertoire of unorthodox moves and ways to score. He saw a guy with ambidextrous ball-handling skills. He saw a guy with a ridiculously long shooting range. He was intrigued.

In fact, Rose and Wardenburg were so intrigued that they traveled across the country to watch Jimmer play football his junior season. And, of course, they came back to watch him play basketball. It was a major commitment in terms of time and expense, but the coaches believed they were recruiting a special talent—and knew they had a great chance to get him.

They just hoped no bigger programs would see the light and jump in on Jimmer late in the process, under-cutting all the work they'd put into recruiting him. They wanted to secure an early commitment before he started his senior season.

High-school basketball seniors have two different peri-ods in which they can sign national letters of intent to at-tend a college and receive a scholarship. The early signing period is in November. The late signing period is in April. Rose and Wardenburg were angling for Jimmer to sign in the early period.

When Jimmer was a senior, he made an official visit to BYU's Provo campus for a home football game weekend in September. He already had familiarity with the campus since Lindsay had gone there, so the visit was less a fact-finding trip than a formality on the way toward a commit-ment to play for the Cougars.

The next week, it was time for BYU to make its home visit to Glens Falls and try to close the deal with a com-mitment. Jimmer and T. J. huddled and decided the family should meet Rose and Wardenburg at Angelina's for dinner and then return to the modest home on Ogden Street for the serious sales pitch.

In the small Fredette basement, the coaches showed a BYU highlight video and laid out their plan for Jimmer. Rose said he foresaw him "running the show" for the Cougars, and the family envisioned him playing point guard and possibly even starting as a freshman. Everyone was excited.

All that was left was for Jimmer to accept the scholarship offer and say he'd sign with BYU in November. A verbal commitment then and there would virtually end the process.

"We were all in the basement," T. J. said. "The coaches were tense. Everyone was waiting for Jimmer to say something, and he really didn't."

The reason: Jimmer was waiting for his uncle Lee, who had worked so diligently with him to improve his game, to arrive. This was a big family moment, and he wanted the key family members present. A guy who loved up-tempo basketball went into an awkward, four-corners stall mode until Lee arrived.

"Finally Jimmer said, 'I've decided to go to BYU,'" T. J. recalled. "Wardenburg jumped off the couch and started celebrating."

Said Kay: "We all hugged and were very excited for him. I think I got teary-eyed for a few minutes, but that's normal for me."

As huge as the commitment was for the BYU coaches,

it scarcely made a ripple in the national recruiting land-scape. Rivals.com, one of the major recruiting websites, devoted all of two paragraphs to the news. The world of college basketball treated Jimmer's commitment to play at BYU as a ho-hum event.

The increasingly popular (and populated) world of col-lege recruiting is a heavily subjective place. It is governed by the star system: top-level recruits are "five-star" pros-pects, followed by four-star players, then three-star guys and so on. Those rankings are made by recruiting ana-lysts who travel the country watching players in both high school and AAU settings.

The modern recruiting analyst is much more informed than his predecessors, who often had only limited oppor-tunities to evaluate players. But it's still a very inexact sci-ence, full of misreads of potential, work ethic, and deter-mination. Exhibit A: Jimmer Fredette.

Jimmer was a three-star recruit with one major re-cruiting service and a two-star recruit with the other. He elicited very little buzz from analysts. He was not ranked in the Rivals.com Top 150 national recruits for the Class of 2007—a remarkably talented class. Nor was he in the Scout.com Top 100. Neither service put him among its top point guard recruits either.

In fact, Jimmer wasn't even considered the top pros-pect on the City Rocks AAU team. That was Talor Battle, a point guard from Albany. Battle went on to have an outstanding college career at Penn State, ending up the school's all-time leading scorer—but you didn't see him winning any national Player of the Year awards or hear his name called in the first round of the NBA draft.

Jimmer's name was prominently mentioned in both categories. After his stellar college career, while traveling around picking up some of that Player of the Year hardware, Jimmer would bump into such guys as Villanova coach Jay Wright or Notre Dame coach Mike Brey—Big East coaches who passed on him out of high school.

Their common refrain: "How did we miss you?"

CHAPTER EIGHT

CHANGE

Two weeks into Jimmer's freshman season at BYU, he staged an uncharacteristic act of noncompliance. He came out for practice one day wearing a white jersey, although he was regularly on the blue team. In Dave Rose's program, the starting five plus top substitutes wear blue reversible jerseys at practice. The other players turn the jerseys inside out and wear white. It is solely up to the coaches to decide who wears what color.

Jimmer's college career had gotten off to a good start—through the Cougars' first four games, all victories, he came off the bench but was playing and contributing. He was averaging more than 11 points, with a high game of 19, and playing half the game. But when BYU went to Las Vegas for a tournament against tougher competition, Jimmer's playing time was suddenly curtailed. He played just 12 scoreless minutes in an upset of Louisville

Kay holding Jimmer the day he was born.

T. J. holding Jimmer for the first time.

Jimmer looking through the window at
Lindsay and T. J. skating in the backyard.

Jimmer, age 2, with Al.

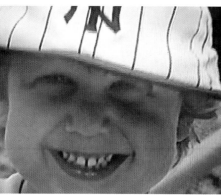

Jimmer, age 2, at a New York Yankees game.

Jimmer after playing basketball
with T. J. in their backyard.

Jimmer, age 4, playing in a basketball league for 7- to 9-year-olds at East Field in Glens Falls.

T. J., age 12, having fun with Jimmer, age 5.

The Fredette family at a friend's house in Glens Falls in the early 1990s.

T. J. helping Jimmer, age 5, to shoot hoops.

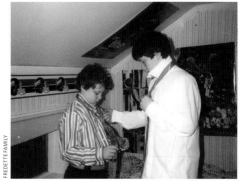
T. J. coaching Jimmer in tie tying.

Jimmer on his fifth birthday in the
living room with his first hoop.

Jimmer and Lindsay at the end of year
concert at their elementary school.

Jimmer as the water boy at one of T. J.'s high school games.

Jimmer, age 12, playing baseball in his basketball high-tops.

Jimmer's high school team after a big win.

Lindsay, T. J., and Al standing beside the memorial stone at the dedication of the field named after Kay's father, Clinton Taft, a coaching legend in Whitehall, New York.

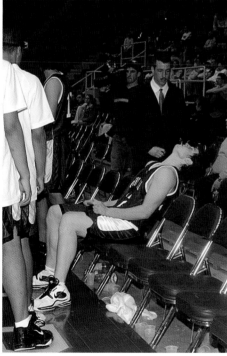

Jimmer after a two-point loss in the sectional finals.

Jimmer wearing number 32 and running the football as a junior in high school.

T. J. coaches Jimmer through his first shave.

T. J. next to Jimmer graffiti in Glens Falls.

BYU coaches visit Jimmer during his senior year of high school.
At Angelina's restaurant, Jimmer verbally commits to play at BYU.

I James T Fredette agree on this day Jan 27, 2007 to do the (date) work and make the neccessary sacrifices to be able to reach my ultimate goal of playing in the NBA

Signature   Witness

The contract.

Jimmer goes up for a jump shot
during a sectionals game.

Jimmer and uncle Lee Taft after a workout in the off-season from BYU.

Jimmer signing an autograph after a big BYU win over Arizona.

Jimmer going up for a shot during an MWC tournament game.

Jimmer and Kay at a Real Salt Lake soccer game.

Jimmer after the BYU win over San Diego State at the Marriott Center.

Jimmer holding a piece of the
BYU champs' winning net.

Jimmer's recognitions. *Left to right from top:*
Lowe's Senior CLASS Award; Adolph Rupp Award;
NABC Division 1 Player of the Year Award.
Bottom: Wooden Award; Naismith Award; AP Player
of the Year Award; Oscar Robertson Award.

Jimmer and Whitney in their BYU uniforms.

T. J. performing at the Marriott Center before the BYU game against San Diego State.

Jimmer in the Lake Tahoe Celebrity Golf tournament, July 2011. He was paired with Charles Barkley and Tim Tebow, among others.

T. J. playing in his first basketball tournament at Crandall Park in Glens Falls after two years of battling back from a debilitating vestibular and neurological malfunction following a routine ACL operation. "Team Fredette" won the tournament.

Jimmer with Justin Timberlake: (left) in 1998 in Louisiana at sister Lindsay's Miss Teen USA pageant where Justin performed with *NSync and (right) in 2011 when Justin presented Jimmer with an ESPY award.

Jimmer accepting the 2011 ESPY Award in Los Angeles, California, on July 13, 2011.

Jimmer waiting for his name to be called at the NBA draft.

Jimmer shaking David Stern's hand after his name was called as the number 10 pick in the 2011 NBA draft. Sacramento later announced their trade with Milwaukee for Jimmer to join the Kings.

Jimmer posing for the world with his Kings jersey.

Jimmer's NBA draft party cake made by Cake Boss.

T. J. has never outgrown his boyhood greeting of stroking Jimmer's face.

Jimmer and Whitney announce their engagement in August 2011.

Jimmer and Whitney on their wedding day, June 1, 2012, in Denver, Colorado.

The Fredette family in front of the LDS Denver Colorado Temple on Jimmer and Whitney's wedding day. *From left:* T. J., Kay, Jimmer, Whitney, Al, Lindsay, and her husband, Brent Peterson.

Rookie Jimmer living the dream.

and then five scoreless minutes in a close loss to North Carolina.

After that trip Jimmer came out wearing a white jersey so he could play against the blue team and show how well he would do against the starters. He was sending a message to his coaches. He wanted to play against the starters to prove he deserved more playing time.

Head coach, Dave Rose, said, "Jimmer, you're blue."

"No, Coach," he responded. "I'm white."

Rose pulled aside his uber-competitive point guard and said, "Sorry, Jimmer. Work with me here—you're blue. You're just going to have to be patient."

Up to that point, basketball had been the easy part of the college experience. The college transition had been hard enough off the court.

The distance from Glens Falls to Provo is 2,229 miles, from Northeast to Rocky Mountain West. Just about everything changes from upstate New York to Utah, including the demographics of the people. In Glens Falls, Mormons are a tiny minority. In Provo, they are the dominant majority.

Jimmer is a teetotaler, but he was accustomed to going to parties where some of his friends and peers drank alcohol. Some smoked marijuana. In Provo, parties were almost uniformly sober events.

On Sundays in Provo, the entire town went to church and otherwise shut down. That was never the case back home.

And as is often the case in a college town, there were plenty of kids living well off their parents' money. Jimmer and most of his friends from Glens Falls grew up modestly and worked for whatever was in their wallets.

"I feel like people's mind-sets are different [between his hometown and Provo]," Jimmer said. "I don't know how to say it, but Glens Falls is a place where people work really hard for their money. A real blue-collar place. Out there it's different. A lot of people own their own businesses. They work hard but in a different way."

Jimmer had arrived in Provo in a bit of a rush—the day after his high school graduation in June, he headed west. The next day, summer workouts were underway. Most other freshmen had graduated at an earlier date and had some transition time to get ready for college, but not Jimmer.

Upon their arrival on campus in the summer of 2007, all the players were immersed in Coach Rose's rigorous conditioning program. The workouts were harder than anything the players had done in high school. Even Jimmer, despite the work he'd done with his uncle, was not ready for the increased aerobic demands. The air was thin, given Provo's 4,551-foot elevation. The culture was also different. Jimmer missed home and family.

He was a natural homebody, accustomed to having family around him. He'd traveled on the AAU summer basketball circuit, but Al was almost always with him on those trips. Jimmer wasn't a go-out-and-see-the-world kind of guy, but suddenly he had been thrust into a new and foreign part of it.

"It was tough on him, and it was very tough on us," Kay Fredette said. "I cried for months before he left because I just couldn't believe he had to go that far away from us. He was my last child. It was tough on T. J. also to see his little brother go off on his own where he wouldn't be able to see him every day. He was always so protective of him."

Jimmer's summer roommate was Michael Loyd, a fellow guard on the basketball team. Loyd had his own circle of friends, though, and was rarely in the dorm. Jimmer, who tends to be shy until he gets to know people, spent a lot of time alone.

One Sunday afternoon shortly after he arrived in BYU, Jimmer called home and told his dad, "I don't have anything to eat." School was out, so the dining hall at the Cannon Center was closed, and Jimmer's meal card was useless. Since it was a Sunday in Provo, all the restaurants within walking distance of campus were closed—and Jimmer didn't have a car. He didn't have much cash, either, and when he scraped up enough to hit the vending machines he found that they had all been cleaned out.

"He was really down," Al Fredette recalled. "He was alone, beat up, tired, hungry."

Salvation arrived unexpectedly. Jimmer's uncle Dennis and aunt Susan were living in Sandy at the time, about 35 minutes north of Provo. Dennis and his family were

driving home from a Shakespeare Festival and while passing through Provo called Jimmer to invite him to eat dinner with them.

"It picked up from there," Al said.

Eventually, Jimmer settled in at Merrill Hall with roommate and teammate Nick Martineau, and also bonded with
Provo product and fellow teammate Chris Collinsworth.
The three had a similar sense of humor and similar tastes
in movies and TV. Most days they'd watch comedies:
Everybody Loves Raymond and *King of Queens* and *Seinfield*
and *Family Guy*. Then, when those were over, it was time
to watch sports.

And debate. For the first half of the year, before they
even had a TV, Jimmer and his friends spent their time arguing—about everything. Sports debates were common. A
friend who was a goalkeeper on the BYU soccer team one
day stated that soccer goalies are better athletes than basketball players. You can imagine how well that went over.

Jimmer said, "You've got to be kidding. That guy
doesn't even have to do much. You can't say he's more
athletic than LeBron James." That debate went on for a
long time. "He got so into it that he just wanted to win
the argument at one point. He knew it wasn't true, but he
was arguing because he wanted to. He was just arguing for
fun."

There weren't just interactions with soccer players and
other athletes in student housing. At BYU there are no
athletic dorms, and that means the jocks are integrated

with the regular kids on a daily basis. That's a departure from a lot of the big-college athletic programs, but what BYU provides is far from the normal student-athlete experience. And Jimmer was fine with that. He and Martineau were the only basketball players in their dorm his freshman year.

"I think it was great to show everybody athletes are regular people," he said. "We're just normal guys that play sports and like to have a good time. It was fun."

They were normal guys at an abnormal school for athletes. BYU is like no other place that competes at the highest level of NCAA sports.

Kay Fredette loved the fact that a vast percentage of the BYU students were regular churchgoers. And since the Cougars basketball team did not play games on Sundays—unlike every other school in the country—Sundays were for going to church services, which Jimmer enjoyed doing.

"I am a firm believer in keeping your spiritual side intact because it will help you in all aspects of your life," Kay said. "I think it has helped all of my kids in their lives. They know that there is more to life than just basketball and whatever else they are interested in. Spirituality is the key to happiness and keeping a balance in your life. Everyone needs that."

The big religious question for Jimmer was whether he would go on a mission, which is considered a rite of passage and a religious obligation by many members of the LDS faith. According to church reports, there were more than 52,000 missionaries serving worldwide in 2010, most of whom were young men who had taken two years off school and accepted an assignment from church leaders to live around the globe to spread their faith. Such missions are expected of young LDS men who are physically and mentally able to serve, though such service is always voluntary and dependent on individual circumstances. The expectation for young women is not as great, but they too may opt to serve missions.

BYU's athletic teams are full of players who took time away from school for missionary service. It is widely considered one of the reasons why the Cougar athletic teams are so successful—because players return to school more physically and emotionally mature. Competing as a 24- or 25-year-old against teenagers can be an advantage.

But with players coming and going so often, it also can wreak havoc with a team's chemistry and continuity. Coaches must adjust rosters annually, and missionaries must work to scrape the rust off their athletic abilities when they return.

For Jimmer, the decision regarding missionary service was different than for many of his peers and predecessors. For one thing, despite his relatively modest recruitment, he believed he had a future as a professional basketball player. Given the narrow window of time during which a pro basketball player has to make a living, delaying that is a risk. For another, Jimmer really didn't have a frame of reference for what a mission would be like—the rewards or the drawbacks.

"A lot of people grow up dreaming about going on a mission, but when I was younger, I didn't even think about that," Jimmer said. "My dad never went on a mission. My brother never went on a mission. So, I didn't know anybody who had really gone on a mission. I just never thought about it.

"Then all of a sudden, when I was eighteen, my dad asked me, 'Have you ever thought about going on a mission?' I said, 'To be honest with you, no, I haven't really.' I talked to people about it, and I prayed about it and definitely took it very seriously, but I never got a strong urge, telling me to go out and do it. So, you know, I thought maybe it's just best for me to try to help the church in other ways."

That stance was supported by many but opposed by a few. As Jimmer's fame grew, some LDS members believed a mission would be the perfect statement to make about his priorities. He received critical mail and feedback from some church members who thought he was abdicating his duty and from others who wondered whether he'd committed some grave sin that was keeping him from being extended a call.

Others believed the opposite—that Jimmer in a BYU uniform, bringing attention to the school and its values, was the best way to be an ambassador for the LDS religion. They believed that using basketball as his platform served more good than any amount of door-to-door mission work could accomplish.

"I've been kind of a goodwill ambassador for the church and probably done more than anything else that I ever could have done going out and knocking on doors, because I've reached so many people just by talking about it in the media," Jimmer said. "People wonder about it, and that helps other missionaries get into the door a lot of times, if they can relate. So, I think that it was the right decision for me."

Kay and Al actually had a brief experience of their own at BYU, dating all the way back to the 1970s. After working those hard years in the paper mill in Glens Falls, Al decided he'd go back to school to improve his education and get a better job. He envisioned himself becoming a lawyer.

As a Mormon convert, he decided he'd try going to BYU. He moved across country to picturesque Provo and enrolled. He'd found some roommates to defer costs, with the understanding that Kay would follow him soon thereafter. The sticking point for the childless couple was their two large dogs—Kay wasn't going to part with them, and Al was sure no apartment manager would let her keep them in BYU student housing.

"I remember saying to him, 'Oh, yeah? Watch me!'" Kay recalled. "I was coming across the country with those two dogs, like it or not. How could I give them away? It wasn't going to happen.

"I always go by the motto, 'Where there's a will, there's

a way.' I had a very strong will. Sure enough, I found a place, much to Al's surprise, right down the street from where he was staying."

The apartment was located within walking distance to campus and spacious enough for the young couple and their two dogs. Al had to laugh and shake his head at his wife's determination.

They spent a happy semester at BYU—Al studying and making good grades, Kay running the dogs up to campus and staying busy with other projects. They went home at the end of that spring semester with the intention of going back in the fall. But Al was approached with a good job offer, one he didn't think he should pass up, and the Fredettes never returned to BYU as students.

But the experience there was positive enough that they sent two of their three children to BYU. Lindsay was first, going there to study dance. She liked the area so much that she stayed, earning her degree in dance from BYU, a master's degree from the University of Utah in movement analysis, and then a degree in elementary education. She lives near Salt Lake City with her husband, Brent Peterson, and their two young children.

That was the other saving grace for Jimmer during his time at BYU. Lindsay was just up Interstate 15 from Provo. The two siblings had grown up many years apart, but as kids they rarely had the typical brother-sister clash. Jimmer did complain at first when Lindsay practiced the violin in the little house on Ogden Street, but she quickly got much better, and she ended up playing for nine years. Lindsay complained once in a while when Jimmer tried to include himself in something she might be doing, but there was never any fighting between them.

And absence can make the heart grow fonder. That, and the inevitable growing up process. Lindsay did miss her little brother, who was only ten when she went away to college. Whenever she came home from BYU or the U of U, she would take Jimmer to play miniature golf at one of the tourist traps in Lake George, New York, just up the road from Glens Falls. Those golf outings became their tradition.

When Jimmer got to BYU, the two could finally begin having a fully formed relationship. He was in the area and needed the familial support, and she could relate to him much better as a young adult than as a hyperactive young boy.

"I was glad I was able to be out here and help him," Lindsay said. "I think just knowing that he had someone if he needed it was helpful. We always had a relationship, but since he's been out here, we've become friends, which with an age difference like ours between siblings, you don't always get. So, it's fun now.

"He is, I would say, more quiet as a young adult. He still has that funny side to him, and he'll still joke around and goof off. But he's also more mature. Whenever he talks about his plans, his life, he's very thoughtful, a lot more quiet and reserved. He would still rather goof off than talk about something serious, but that makes him fun to be around. And that kid-like nature has helped him deal with all the pressure he's experienced."

Of their relationship, Jimmer said, "I've gotten to know Lindsay so much better. We hung out a lot while I was in college, and she helped me out a lot. Anything I needed, she would help out. She was really, really helpful that way and helped me not be as homesick.

"She is also a very loving person. And she's fun to be around. She thinks she's funny. She's not as funny as she thinks she is, but it's that she thinks she's funny that's pretty funny—know what I mean? She's fun to joke with—you can joke with her, and she doesn't ever get offended or anything."

What does offend Lindsay is sitting in the stands at a game and hearing other fans criticize her baby brother. When she started attending Jimmer's BYU games and heard some of the trash talk directed at him, the Fredette family temper flared a few times.

"She's gotten into a couple of different arguments with other fans," Jimmer said. "When people get on me, she'll be the first one to start yelling at people—she and T. J. and my parents—trying to calm them down is pretty funny."

During Jimmer's freshman year, the Fredette family probably wanted to have a few words with Dave Rose, too. After scoring so many points in high school, there was a new reality on the basketball court. The playing time that was curtailed early in the season against Louisville and North Carolina was sporadic for a long time thereafter.

While recruiting Jimmer, Rose had said he wanted him to "run the show" at BYU. To the Fredettes, that sounded as though he was being promised a starting point guard job. But it didn't work that way at first, as Jimmer sought to fit into Rose's playing style.

Rose liked to play at a fast tempo, which fit Jimmer's mentality just fine. But Coach Rose's offensive philosophy was all about passing the ball into the post and around the perimeter without it stopping in one guy's hands for a long period of time. Rose wasn't big on guards who spent a lot of time dribbling and penetrating—which were precisely Jimmer's strong suits.

BYU was movement without the ball: cut, catch, and shoot. Jimmer was into possessing the ball and creating off the dribble. He didn't fit Rose's idea of a point guard, so he found himself backing up both starting guards—and both of them were seniors.

"I had a problem with it at first, for sure," Jimmer said.

So the promising start was something of a false start. The 25 minutes he'd played in the season-opening game November 10 against Long Beach State would be the most playing time he would see until late February. The 19 points he scored on Hartford November 20 would be his season high.

Unlike so many of the freshmen who become instant-impact players in modern college hoops, Jimmer had to wait in line to star. He didn't arrive in Provo with blue-chip, All-American hype, or a posse of hangers-on and advisers who had anything invested in his immediate stardom. He came off the bench as a freshman and averaged just 7 points and 19 minutes per game that year.

"We had a pretty good team with a great point guard," Coach Dave Rose said. "We had to figure out whether Jimmer'd be a better shooting guard or point guard, and the guys in front of him were redshirt seniors. We played him as a back-up to both."

The starting point guard, Ben Murdock, hurt his ankle at New Mexico February 26. That provided Jimmer with one of his best opportunities in months to show what he could do.

In a crazed road atmosphere and a close conference game, he stepped up to the occasion. He made a steal, dived in on a loose ball, hit a couple of shots, and made a key assist. BYU escaped The Pit with a 70–69 overtime win that had Jimmer's fingerprints all over it.

"I kind of made some real big plays at the end," he said. "I was so excited and all the seniors were so excited that I had come in and helped them so well. It was a cool experience for me because all the guys in front of me who were seniors were cheering for me and that was kind of my breakthrough game. Then I just kept playing through the rest of the year. I was always on blue after that."

CHAPTER NINE

RISE

Before going home at the end of his freshman year at BYU, Jimmer went to Dave Rose's office. He asked his coach a simple question: "What do I need to do to be your point guard next year?"

Rose was glad to hear the question. He knew by the end of Jimmer's first season that he could be a special talent—and after initially resisting some of the coaching he got and chafing at his place in the playing rotation, this question showed that Jimmer was willing to adapt and put in the work to get better. Rose told Jimmer to work on ball handling and thinking more like a true point guard—getting teammates involved and being a vocal leader.

Jimmer took it all in and went back to Glens Falls with a mission—to become a college starter. He went to the high school every day and worked toward that end. He did strength-and-speed training with his uncle Lee and sometimes had someone rebound for him when he shot, but most of the actual basketball drills were on his own.

That's the way Jimmer has always liked it. He'd scrimmage with a group, but when working on the fine points of his game, he preferred to be alone—an approach he felt had its creative benefits. A 2012 *New York Times* story noted an academic study of computer programmers at 92 different companies that showed productivity was strongly correlated to having privacy in the workplace. As Picasso once said, "Without great solitude, no serious work is possible."

Jimmer found his solitude in the gym. That solitude made the conversations with himself easier to hear.

Yes, conversations with himself.

"I'm sure, if some people have seen me in the gym, they probably think I'm crazy," Jimmer admitted. "I'll definitely sometimes yell at myself and get on my case and make sure I'm going as hard as I can. I'd yell at myself, 'You've gotta stay focused,' or, 'You're losing focus.' It's hard to do, but if you can do it, it's really effective. I'm definitely talking to myself about different moves and different things. Trash-talking myself, too, you know, just trying to keep myself motivated. I definitely talk to myself a lot."

What does Jimmer trash-talking himself sound like?

"It's like, 'Come on, man, you're the *worst* basketball player.' After you make a stupid mistake, or you're trying to perfect a move and it's just not working for you, and then you're thinking, 'Gosh, why are you so *bad* at basketball?' But then you eventually get it, and then you say to yourself, 'Good move, Jim. Good move.'"

During the summer of 2008, Jimmer cajoled, trashtalked, and worked himself into being a better player—a more confident, better toned, and well-conditioned player. A college basketball starter capable of fulfilling the recruiting promise to "run the show" at BYU as a sophomore.

There was, of course, a difference between *running* the show and *being* the show. The Cougars still had a couple of upperclassmen who were the focal points of the offense—junior post man Jonathan Tavernari and senior swingman Lee Cummard. Over the course of the 2008–09 season they each took more shots than Jimmer—but they didn't play more minutes. And as the season wore on, Jimmer began to exert more and more influence over the offense.

By the end of his sophomore season, his scoring average had more than doubled from 7 as a freshman to 16.2 points per game. He also led the Cougars in assists and steals and was second in scoring. BYU tied for the Mountain West Conference title.

But another successful BYU season ended on another unfulfilling note: For the second straight season, the Cougars were eliminated in the first round of the NCAA tournament by Texas A&M. The school's streak without so much as a single NCAA tourney win was now fifteen years and counting.

With leading scorer Cummard graduated, Rose had a

decision to make with his 2009–10 team: keep the same offense and run everything through Tavernari, a high-volume shooter who didn't make a great percentage of his shots? Or, break the mold and turn the team over to his most talented player, Jimmer, even though he wasn't a senior? Rose chose to break the mold.

"I was glad and maybe even a little surprised they made a change," Jimmer said. "Because some coaches don't like to change. Some coaches just say, 'Run this the way that we run it, and either you like it or you don't.' But these guys changed the way we played—real up-tempo and a lot of different motions to get the guards coming off screens and get us in good positions to score."

Knowing the changes that were coming for his junior year, Jimmer went home to Glens Falls with a plan. He set an even more rigorous and ambitious workout schedule for himself to be ready for a breakout season to come.

"I thought I was right there because I was first-team all-conference," Jimmer said. "Not many sophomores had done that in the conference. I knew that the next year it would be my team, and I would be the leader on the team. I would be able to go in and do what I needed to do. I knew that the coaches were giving me the reins at that point—that was a big thing for me."

Shortly after he got back to the house on Ogden Street for the summer, Jimmer went up into his tiny bedroom and wrote down his goals for his junior year at BYU. He'd never done that before—other than signing "The

Contract," of course, which was still posted on the wall above his bed. But until now, he'd never gotten specific about his aspirations for a single season.

Jimmer didn't show his goal sheet to anyone—just folded it up and set it on the table next to his bed. The list:

- Make at least third-team All-American
- Win a third straight Mountain West Conference championship
- Win a game in the NCAA tournament for the first time
- Win a game at UNLV for the first time
- Average 21 points and five assists per game

There was one other goal he didn't put on paper but kept in the back of his mind.

"I wanted to be NBA-ready by the end of my junior year," he said. "That was what my goal was. Not many people knew that goal. I didn't tell many people."

Give the guy credit for finishing what he set out to do: Jimmer was a third-team All-American; the Cougars won an NCAA tourney game for the first time since 1993; and Jimmer averaged 22.1 points and 4.7 assists. The only things he didn't check off the list were a victory at UNLV and an MWC crown—BYU finished one game behind New Mexico and lost to the Runnin' Rebels in the finals of the MWC tournament.

But that was the season when the world started to

take note of the guard with the quirky game and funny name. Jimmer had eight games of 20 or more points before Christmas his junior season, but it wasn't until he exploded for 49 points, nine assists, and seven rebounds against high-profile Arizona on December 28 that his reputation went national. From that point forward, college basketball fans were increasingly intrigued.

As fate would have it, Jimmer was felled by mononucleosis shortly thereafter. He sat out two games completely and played sparingly in two others, recovering for the conference stretch run. When his strength came back, so did his scoring: 33 at San Diego State; 36 against arch rival Utah; 36 at Colorado State. When Jimmer scored a total of 75 points in the final two games of the Mountain West Conference tournament, it stamped him as one of the must-watch players in the 2010 NCAA tournament.

But how long would the Cougars be in it this time? Another first-round loss would give Jimmer short shelf life as a national curiosity.

Their first-round opponent was Florida, a team that had won national titles in 2006 and 2007. BYU was a No. 7 seed to Florida's No. 10, but many observers favored the household-name Gators over a still-mysterious team from a lower-profile league and an overlooked time zone.

On the afternoon of March 18, in the first game of the day in Oklahoma City, the casual fans in America were introduced to Jimmer. They watched him score 37 points in a 99–92 double overtime victory over Florida. They watched him handle the ball against pressure defense for 46 withering minutes, until his legs nearly gave out beneath him. They watched him score in a variety of unorthodox ways—scoop shots and leaners and floaters and layups from the hip, all variations on moves he had learned in the backyard on Ogden Street while trying to score on T. J. and the other older kids in the neighborhood.

BYU would not have won the game without an improbable 26 points off the bench from Michael Loyd, but this was the Jimmer Show. He was the focal point of Florida's defense, and still the Gators could not stop him.

When it was over, an exhausted but ebullient Jimmer ran to the stands and embraced Kay, Al, and T. J.

"You did it, baby," T. J. told him.

"I dreamed about this as a young child," Jimmer told the national media when it was over, perhaps thinking back to those days watching the state high school tournaments in the Glens Falls Civic Center.

For one shining moment, Jimmer was the leading man of March. He was the face of the tournament at the precise time when America's casual college basketball fans take notice. For the next 48 hours, Jimmer Mania went viral.

Everyone heard about T. J.'s rap song about his brother, "Amazing." Tales of the prison games began to spread. He was a fresh story—Obscure Shooter from Utah Lights Up March Madness As Rapper Brother Rejoices!—and the media ate it up.

Unfortunately for Jimmer, the hoopla also sharpened

the resolve of second-round opponent Kansas State to stop him. The second-seeded Wildcats had excellent guards capable of harassing him on the perimeter and athletic big men capable of deterring his drives into the paint.

It was the quintessential bad matchup. Coming off that exhausting double-overtime game, Jimmer was held to 21 points in a 12-point loss to Kansas State. But at least BYU had finally gotten out of the first round—and America would have Jimmer on its radar heading into his senior season.

If there was going to be a senior season.

That secret goal Jimmer had about being NBA ready? He was prepared to find out how close he came to achieving it when the season was over. To the surprise of some, he entered his name in the 2010 NBA draft.

Many people figured this was just a preliminary test of the waters and that Jimmer would quickly withdraw and return to school. The doubters viewed him as a Great White Hope who scored on volume shooting in a user-friendly offense and would be exposed in the pro game— especially defensively. They'd seen this movie before with high-scoring college stars who could not make the transition athletically to the pros.

But Jimmer was serious about it, and there was more interest from the NBA than many observers expected. He worked out for a few teams to favorable reviews—most notably the Nets, whom Jimmer said told him they would take him with the 27th pick of the first round.

First-round picks get guaranteed contracts. They get paid a phenomenal salary, and the franchises invest time and effort in the players they have to pay. They work to develop their first-round picks, while second-round picks or free agents with smaller salaries might not get as much coaching, attention, and repetitions in practice.

If Jimmer was indeed going to be a first-round pick, he had to strongly consider ending his college career and staying in the draft. BYU fans might not have known how close they came to missing out on the thrilling ride that was Jimmer's senior season.

"I definitely was leaning to going, in the beginning," he said. "Everyone thought I was hot at that point, and everyone was starting to know who I was. And the big thing is that people were thinking, 'This kid could be really good,' but they didn't know much about me. They were just kind of projecting me there. And I thought, 'This could be an opportunity of a lifetime.'"

The decision weighed heavily on him. Every day, Jimmer talked to his girlfriend, Whitney Wonnacott, and to his parents and brother about it. It was the only thing on his mind when he woke up and the only thing on his mind when he went to bed. It would be a life-altering decision that had to be made in a hurry, since the window to test the waters was shorter than ever. The stress was significant.

Jimmer's parents wanted him to return to BYU for his

senior season but were adamant about letting him make his own decision.

"I felt that it would be hard to give up your last year of college to go to a very different type of life," Kay said. "I was on the side of him staying for that last year because it's a time in your life, those college years, that you will never get back again. I knew that he loved the college experience he was having and that it would be hard for him to give that up for the unknown and in some ways difficult life of an NBA player. The thought of the NBA, which was his goal and his dream, was very tempting to him, but I don't think he was really ready to leave BYU just yet. My advice to him was to do what your heart tells you to do."

The advice that resonated most with Jimmer came from former BYU legend and current Boston Celtics general manager Danny Ainge. After working out for Ainge and the Celtics, Jimmer sought the counsel of the leading scorer in BYU history. Ainge told him that his own senior year was one of the best years of his life—not just playing basketball but being in college and enjoying that lifestyle as long as possible.

That input swayed Jimmer a bit. As he weighed the decision in his mind, he settled on a new thought: "I could do better. I could leave a legacy here. Have an unbelievable year."

Funny thing: some people in both the NBA and in Jimmer's camp doubted whether he could have a year any more unbelievable than the one he'd just finished. They suspected he'd about maxed out his marketability.

When it was finally time to make the call, Jimmer relied on his original motivator, coach, confidant, and big brother, T. J. He came out to Provo during that stretch, and on decision day T. J. and Jimmer took a long walk outside while hashing it over.

Finally, Jimmer told T. J. that he planned on pulling his name out of the draft and returning to school.

"That's a good decision," T. J. told him. "But you're going to need to be national Player of the Year now. You're going to have to do that to raise your stock."

T. J. had heard the talk about how Jimmer's stock had maxed out. He wasn't buying it. It seemed a long shot for a player from the Mountain West Conference to win national Player of the Year, especially given the league's TV package—very few of their games were available for national distribution. But nobody believed in Jimmer the way T. J. believed in Jimmer.

"Let's prove them wrong again," T. J. told him.

"All right," Jimmer said.

So the two went into Jimmer's Provo apartment and wrote a fresh set of senior-season goals. Among them: win national Player of the Year.

Monumental decision made, it was time to tell those who had been waiting on tenterhooks. Jimmer went to Rose's office at the Marriott Center. He asked Rose to dial up his parents in Glens Falls and put them on speakerphone.

When the Fredettes came on the line, Jimmer said, "You know what? I'm coming back."

In Glens Falls, Al, Kay, and T. J. could hear Rose whoop with joy. In Rose's office, Jimmer could see the relief and happiness on his coach's face.

"I think it's a great decision," Rose told him, speaking for BYU fans everywhere.

Jimmer also made a prediction to his coach and his parents on the phone that day: "I know people say I'm hot and should go now into the draft and that I'll never have another year like last year, but they are wrong. I can do better, and I will."

A year later, with every major Player of the Year award in Jimmer's possession, Al could laugh about it. "He called it," Al said.

But as with Jimmer's other goals, just writing it down or saying it aloud didn't make it happen. Hard work made it happen. For the third straight summer, Jimmer returned home and ramped up his workout regimen yet again.

"I was locked in," he said. "I was working out twice a day, every day. I always took Sunday off, but I was *really* locked in. I started working out at a professional level. That's kind of what my uncle wanted to do, because he knew I wanted to be at a professional level at that point. So, I started doing two-a-days—a lot of jump shots, a lot of intense conditioning work. It was definitely a turning point in my training career. I had to turn it up a notch."

At the same time, T. J.'s physical and mental problems were turning up a notch as well. Jimmer was so immersed in his basketball world that he didn't even know that his beloved brother was locked in a fight for his life.

CHAPTER TEN

FALL

As Jimmer's star ascended in the West, T. J. Fredette was not well in the East. The jarring contrast in their fortunes was enough to make the older brother feel the only twinge of jealousy he ever had toward his little brother.

"I couldn't help but feel anger towards God," T. J. wrote, "for allowing me to be stricken with such an affliction while my brother was living out his dreams."

T. J. wrote a lot during those dark days—he wrote lyrics, and he even started writing a book. The subject was the jarring juxtaposition of fortunes for himself and the little brother he had helped set on a path toward greatness.

In his own words, T. J. described the night of February 28, 2009, as a basketball passion play unfolded in two separate gyms on opposite sides of the country:

"It is truly amazing to see how life can present such extreme circumstances of both pleasure and pain. On a cold winter's night at the foot of the beautiful, snow-capped mountains that rise above Provo, Utah, 22,000-plus screaming Cougar fans packed the Marriott Center on the Brigham Young University campus for a basketball showdown between BYU and the Utes of the University of Utah. Another edition of one of the greatest intrastate rivalries in all of college sports was set to take place amidst an atmosphere built for athletic royalty in the Beehive State. Nothing short of spectacular was the scene as the electricity ran through the building like power lines.

"As the excitement continued to build, the players from the BYU Cougars took the floor in front of their roaring, die-hard fans. The Marriott Center's booming sound system pumped out music of triumph and inspiration as the players began their intense pregame warm-up routine.

"The fans were now all on their feet. The student section was in a frenzy, pounding their chests, stamping their feet, and chanting simultaneous cheers at the top of their lungs. Anticipation was converted to pure energy as the building took on the aura of a Roman Colosseum where gladiators were soon to engage in a no-holds-barred battle. This was a battle of basketball. The stage was finally set. What extreme pleasure and exhilaration the BYU basketball players must have felt at that moment in front of such an overwhelming crowd of faith-driven supporters.

"One of the BYU players filled with joy that cold night was a 20-year-old sophomore from Glens Falls, N.Y., named James Taft Fredette, better known to the rest of the world solely as 'Jimmer.'

As Jimmer vigorously prepared for the exciting task laid before him, more than 2,000 miles away, clear across the country in upstate New York, in a gym so tiny that the three-point lines on the opposite ends of the floor overlapped, a warm-up of a much different significance was taking place simultaneously. The atmosphere in this gym was completely the opposite of the electrifying atmosphere in the Marriott Center that evening. The setting in this gym was one of struggle and near-silence. The only sound that could be heard coming from this gym was the occasional dribbling of a deflated basketball that never made its way toward the rim. In this gym, a 26-year-old man wobbled his way up and down the gym floor, struggling just to keep his balance. With his head spinning, blood pressure dropping, and legs randomly shaking, fatigue became an opposing factor with each step he took.

"Making it from one side of the tiny gym to the other would be a task most healthy 26-year-old males could do about 50 times without breaking a sweat. For this man, however, who appeared to be healthy, even to most doctors, making his way across the gym floor just one time was a troublesome challenge. With a basketball in his hand, staying on his feet was the mission, but to actually dribble the ball was an added bonus. Slowly half-stepping down the court with the occasional anti-rhythmic bounce of the partially deflated basketball, in a gym too small to accommodate even a 4-on-4 game, was such a far cry from swooping athletically to the basket, decked out in top-of-the-line Nike warm-up apparel, mentally and physically preparing for a larger-than-life Division I NCAA basketball game. . . .

"The man who was struggling in this little gym in up-state New York was me, Timothy James Fredette, better known to my family as 'T. J.' and known to most people in Provo as Jimmer's brother."

On the night T. J. wrote about, he closed his eyes and pretended, for a brief moment, that he was with Jimmer in a BYU uniform. That he was warming up alongside his brother amid the excitement and fanfare in Provo. That he was getting ready to play the big game with thousands of people watching.

Then he opened his eyes to the reality around him. He was still in the tiny gym in upstate New York. Still suffering from the vestibular disorder that had made his life an unsteady nightmare. First the childhood anxiety, and now this. But at least there was momentary salvation nearby.

When T. J.'s mini-workout was over, he walked across the hall into a room where a TV had been hooked to a satellite cable that would beam Jimmer's game to the Fredettes and family friends. Since so many BYU games were hard to find on-air, the satellite TV at the Mormon church became a conduit to Jimmer—and a lifeline for T. J.

His family saved him the best seat, right in front of the TV. And when the game tipped off, T. J. was able to lose himself in the excitement of watching his little brother. Every dribble, every shot, every movement Jimmer made, T. J. followed with a mind suddenly free from chaos and confusion.

"It was a distraction that somehow helped to lessen my agony," T. J. said. "My brother was helping me in ways he didn't even know."

T. J. had needed the help ever since he awoke from surgery for a partially torn anterior cruciate ligament in his left knee. He was 24 years old, out of college, working at Angelina's, and doing other odd jobs but still playing ball whenever possible. In fact, he was playing the best of his life, toying with the idea of getting a tryout for the NBA's Developmental League, a minor-league system.

Playing in a men's basketball league at the YMCA one day, T. J. went in for a layup, was undercut by a defender, and injured his left knee. He waited a couple of weeks to play again, hoping the pain and weakness would go away, but when he went back to the gym, he tweaked it again and knew the knee would require surgery.

When it was time to repair the damage, doctors put him under full anesthesia for the fairly routine surgery. But T. J. came out of it feeling extremely dizzy and disoriented. And the uncomfortable feeling never went away.

Of all the physical gifts human beings take for granted, an innate sense of balance ranks high on the list. Waking up and getting out of bed, walking down the street, exercising, traveling in virtually any mode of automated transport—those things can all become arduous when your inner ear, brain, and eyes are not in sync.

Every day, T. J. was weak. Shaky. Unsteady on his feet. He described a "dumping feeling" when he stood up, as if part of his body was staying behind or falling back down. He spent days at a time on the couch, waiting for the symptoms to subside.

Eventually T. J. started feeling a little better and began doing his knee rehab work. There were still headaches, but he was able to get up and function for longer periods of time. Then one day he was working out, doing pushups. When he was finished, he stood up abruptly and went right back down, flat on the ground. The room spun, and it took T. J. about half an hour simply to stand up and go home.

The next day was more of the same: spinning rooms, loss of balance, inability to take more than a step or two without feeling as though he were going to fall. It stayed that way for about a year.

T. J. went to a parade of doctors—several neurosurgeons; two ear, nose, and throat specialists; twice to an audiologist; and even to a heart doctor—none of whom could figure out exactly what ailed him. Some didn't even take him seriously, especially when MRIs, MRAs (Magnetic Resonance Angiography, which examines blood vessels), CAT scans, and other examinations of brain function revealed nothing irregular. Friends and associates didn't get it, either.

In addition to the physical symptoms, there was a significant emotional toll on T. J. as well. Normally ebullient and outgoing, he isolated himself at home and withdrew. His self-confidence and self-esteem drained as the weeks went on. He couldn't work and could scarcely write any lyrics for his fledgling rap career.

When he did focus long enough to write down what was in his head, the thoughts were dark and demoralizing.

> *Please don't wake me up*
> *I want to stay in bed*
> *'Cause sleep is the closest thing I have to being*
>   *dead*
> *As soon as I get out of my bed*
> *I feel my head pounding from all the throbbing*
>   *and the pressure*
> *That's why I dread each day, it never ends,*
>   *constantly, it bothers me*
> *I want to be a man that can fight it*
> *But truly, honestly, I'm sick of fighting, sick of*
>   *watching the TV screen*
> *Every step that I take*
> *It's like I'm walking on trampolines*
> *I feel like I'm falling over, it's hard to stay on my*
>   *feet*
> *So I just lay on the couch, and no, I don't want*
>   *to eat*
> *And no, I don't want a visitor*

No, I don't want a listener
I don't want to talk, I'm living like I'm a prisoner
Limited is my freedom, my body's my prison
    guard
My brain is the barbed wire
The walls, bars and yard.

With T. J. in such a dismal state, his parents were distraught. Kay would bottle up her anxiety and then go for long walks, crying the entire way. Then she'd regroup when she came home and try to stay upbeat and strong in T. J.'s presence.

"I used to be a good sleeper, but when he got sick, I don't think I slept much at all," Kay said. "I was not only sad for him but also frustrated because for so long, no one could tell us what was wrong with him. T. J. wasn't the kind of kid who would be making this up. He wanted to be up and moving and a productive member of society, the same as everyone else."

Al handled the concern and anxiety differently, internalizing his stress. He tried his best to fix the problem by scouring for another doctor, another specialist, another expert who could find out what was wrong with his oldest son. They drove all over upstate New York looking for someone who could diagnose T. J.'s problem, and they paid prodigious medical bills—many visits were not covered by insurance, and the testing cost a fortune.

"That was a very hard time," Al said.

Al and Kay tried hard to keep their kids in Utah oblivious to the problem T. J. was experiencing. Lindsay was a young mother, and Jimmer was immersed in academics and basketball. Most every report they got from home was sunny.

But there was no masking the reality of the situation when the family traveled to Utah to see Jimmer play—the infamous, torturous trip for the Wake Forest game in Jimmer's sophomore year, for example. While the family was staying at Lindsay's house, she could tell how much her brother was hurting.

"He had so many days where you could tell he didn't feel well at all," Lindsay said. "Just wasn't himself. It was as though something was being sucked out of him. It was scary."

T. J. did some of his best acting on those trips west, always wanting to seem upbeat around Jimmer. But he couldn't hide everything. On the same trip as the Wake Forest game, the Fredettes drove from Salt Lake to Las Vegas to see BYU play UNLV—a drive T. J. was determined to make.

He'd been disoriented enough at Lindsay's house during that visit that Kay suggested T. J. stay in Salt Lake and watch the game on TV. He wouldn't hear of it—in fact, he wanted to drive himself, since focusing on the road tended to alleviate his symptoms. But the six-hour journey south on I-15 so thoroughly sapped T. J. that he spent most of the game sitting in the stands with his eyes closed.

"This is no way to live," he told Kay during the game.

Jimmer, of course, knew he had the means to make his brother feel better. He wasn't just playing for the joy of the game, for team success, and for personal glory; he was playing to help T. J. endure the toughest days of his life. It was a good thing the kid had broad shoulders, because a lot was being piled on them.

"I just kept in my mind how much he was looking forward to our games," Jimmer said.

After one particularly good game, he texted T. J.: "This one was for you."

"I remember showing my mom the text," T. J. said. "I teared up. That meant so much. It was my only escape from what I was going through."

T. J.'s depression was significant but not considered uncommon. According to the Vestibular Disorders Association, the mental impact is often the biggest problem connected with the disease.

"Even patients who have made an uneasy peace with their symptoms may experience a subtle erosion of self-esteem that arises from a discrepancy between what they think they are and what they believe they should be," wrote Dr. Albert J. Berstein of Vancouver, Washington. "Vestibular patients are always questioning themselves, and it is these questions that cause such damaging stress: Am I making this up? Am I stupid? Am I just lazy?"

T. J. asked himself those questions. Others who knew him probably silently wondered the same thing. Nobody could comprehend the chaos that was raging in his head, and T. J. himself struggled to understand it.

"The difficult thing is that to the outside world, the symptoms I suffer from are invisible," he said. "To the outside world, I look fine. And I go out of my way to make it look as though I'm fine. I didn't want sympathy. I wanted to get better."

The labyrinthine quest to get better finally led, on the suggestion of a fellow church member, to the Vreeland Clinic in Norwich, Vermont. It was a 2½-hour trip across windy roads from Glens Falls, a lurching drive that exacerbated T. J.'s discomfort, but at least there was some potential salvation at the end of the drive.

The Vreeland clinic offered neurologic chiropractic care—similar to what National Hockey League star Sidney Crosby has undergone in his attempt to return to the ice after a series of concussions and other injuries. Dr. Kurt Vreeland and his son, Court, diagnosed T. J.'s vestibular disorder.

"He's in a gray area in terms of health care," Court Vreeland said. "Not really sick, not really well. There's nothing we can see on an MRI or a lab test. Those people end up being diagnosed as depressed or having anxiety. That may be a component of what's wrong—and the anxiety that develops can make the problem worse—but it's a symptom of a deeper issue."

Vreeland said it's unclear whether the anesthesia from the knee surgery caused or worsened any of T. J.'s problems. He believes there is some evidence in his background, dating back to the middle-school anxiety attacks, that indicates the vestibular issue was there all along and perhaps only worsened after surgery.

Vreeland described T. J.'s issue as "a miscommunication in the brain, in the vestibular centers, particularly on the left side." That miscommunication had gone on so long that Vreeland said it lowered the neurological energy on that side of his brain and began to affect T. J.'s blood pressure.

"When a person goes from seated to standing, the blood pressure is supposed to rise," Vreeland said. "We tested T. J., and his blood pressure rose on the left side of his body, as usual, but it dropped on the right side. He was having trouble regulating vision, thought, and motion. His ability to interpret all the information coming to his brain was just off."

So the Vreelands devised a rehabilitation process they were confident would work—but it would take a long time and it would be difficult.

Kay recalled, "I'll never forget what Doctor Vreeland said to T. J., because right then I realized T. J. would be in the fight of his life to become a functional human being. He told T. J., 'The good news is, it's not going to kill you. And the bad news is, it's not going to kill you.'"

Living with it was in fact that difficult at times. Vreeland described the rehab process as similar to watching grass grow in the summer: if you go out and measure it every hour, you won't see much growth. But if you wait a couple of weeks, you will see some progress. He advised T. J. to think "in large chunks of time," such as six months or a year, before expecting to feel noticeably better.

The rehab started with 35 natural supplements a day, plus a prescribed battery of unconventional exercises.

"At first I was thinking, 'This is ridiculous. How is this going to help me get better?'" T. J. recalled.

Vreeland had him wear bright red sunglasses. He had T. J. bounce up and down on a physio ball while trying to read a book. He read an eye chart while turning his head. He spun in a chair—the exercise he liked least. There were regular squirts of water into the ear—sometimes warm, sometimes cold—followed by examinations of T. J.'s pupils. That wasn't much fun, either.

But T. J. stuck to his regimen—he did the exercises every morning, afternoon, and night, about 30 minutes at a time, 90 minutes per day. They were all aimed at desensitizing him to certain movements. For a long time, that was T. J.'s life—watching Jimmer on TV and rehabbing his ravaged vestibular system. Other than two hours twice a week when the Cougars were playing ball, it was a pretty terrible existence—but it was all T. J. had so he kept at it.

"I just put my faith in the doctors," T. J. said. "It got worse at first, but within six or seven months I began living life more the way I want to live it."

After those first tentative workouts at the church gym,

wobbling from one baseline to the other and back, T. J. slowly regained some physical strength and stamina. By the summer after Jimmer's sophomore year, he was able to play hoops with his little brother for a while—each time testing to see if he could play a little longer than the last.

One thing that didn't come back was T. J.'s shooting touch. Jumpers didn't fall very easily and standing still at the foul line sometimes felt like being on the deck of a ship at sea.

"In a way, it's almost like being drunk, I think," T. J. explained.

But missing shots was a whole lot better than missing life while lying on the couch all day. He was able to travel to Utah more easily to see Jimmer play, able to live without a constant, debilitating dizziness.

"He's still not out of the woods," Vreeland said. "But he's doing things he couldn't do two years ago. It's fantastic to see him going from being confined to his house to being able to follow Jimmer around and watch him play."

So Jimmer's growth as a basketball player wasn't the only "amazing" thing happening in the Fredette family. T. J.'s recovery deserved mention in that category as well. Eventually T. J. was able to put his difficulties far enough behind—the childhood anxiety, the adult instability—to perform his music on stage. He still can't fly, however, because the extreme changes in pressure and elevation bother his head tremendously.

FALL

As T. J.'s health improved, so did the mood of his lyrics:

The time passes slowly but at least it passes
I'm trying to look at life through optimistic
*   glasses*
But it's so hard to keep hope when you've
*   suffered so long*
This rehabbing my brain feels like a marathon
It keeps going on and on, I'm trying to persevere
Hearing it gets worse before it gets better is hard
*   to hear*
But I'm still here, I'm seeing a little more clear
Each day I do a little more
I'm fighting the fear
A little less of me staring at walls feeling sorry
Putting all the blame upon God
Like He was trying to harm me
Another chapter of overcoming is coming up
It's a new beginning
All the darkness is dying
I'm back to living
And seeing the light hoping someday I'll be fully
*   cured*
Is the motivation I'm using don't worry if it is
*   blurred*
As long as I see it
I can put my focus on the goal

And know that I'm going to make it
I'm slowly taking control.

Out in Provo, Jimmer was also slowly taking control of the BYU basketball program. Slowly becoming a national name in his sport. Slowly fulfilling the destiny T. J. foresaw and put into writing.

By Jimmer's senior season, he was ready to give his recovering brother something truly joyful to experience.

CHAPTER ELEVEN

PEAK

When the BYU Cougars ran onto the Marriott Center court on November 12, 2010, to open the season against Fresno State, nobody was completely sure what to expect. Optimism was high because Jimmer was back for his senior season and had some veteran teammates around him. But there had been enough personnel losses that doubts remained, and the Cougars hadn't advanced to the NCAA tournament Sweet Sixteen since 1981.

They were unranked in the *USA Today* coaches' poll and No. 23 in the Associated Press poll. Expectations were detectable but hardly huge—except for Jimmer himself.

"I was just thinking, 'I hope he can get through this because there is going to be a ton of pressure on him,'" Al said. "He got lots of preseason awards, and I knew his game was going to be scrutinized heavily. People were saying he's a senior and not in the NBA for a reason—he's no good."

By the time BYU had secured an 83–56 victory over Fresno on opening night, powered by Jimmer's 24 points and eight assists, a season was underway that would captivate a large segment of America's college basketball fans. A lightly recruited guard from small-town New York became a superstar, carrying a team from an off-brand conference to the national top five and the thick of the discussion of national title contenders.

"It was magical," Kay said. "We all had the time of our lives."

Jimmer's primary support came from teammates Jackson Emery and Noah Hartsock, plus sophomore big man Brandon Davies. Jimmer believed that the development of Davies, a 6-foot-9, 235-pound sophomore, was especially important for BYU to be able to compete inside against the best teams in the country.

When Davies began making strides during preseason pickup games and workouts, Jimmer was convinced the season could be one of the best in school history. The parts were all coming together, and the players were working harder than ever.

"I knew we had a good core group of guys coming back who were really experienced, and the only thing that was a concern to me was our big guy situation," Jimmer said. "But the thing was, Brandon was really good, and I knew that he was really good. So, we needed to make sure that he had that confidence. But the problem was, we didn't really have much of a backup center for Brandon. And Brandon sometimes tended to get into foul trouble. That was my biggest concern.

"But I *knew* that we could be really, really good. I didn't know that we could be number three in the country good, but I knew that we had a good shot to be a Top Ten team."

That took a while. It wasn't until the Cougars reached 16–1 in early January that they cracked the Top Ten. As a team from the Mountain West Conference, outside the big-six leagues that get most of the attention and adulation, nothing was given to BYU.

By the time the Cougars achieved that lofty ranking, there already had been some highlight moments.

In early December, BYU played the Jimmer Homecoming Game against Vermont in Glens Falls. At the Civic Center where a young Jimmer dreamed of high school glory—and then achieved it—he came back for one more game in front of the home fans. Jimmer scored 26 points before an adoring sellout crowd as the Cougars remained undefeated.

"People were talking about the Glens Falls game for months," Al recalled. "Coach Rose said that was the best he'd seen a kid do in a homecoming game."

Three days later, back in Utah, Jimmer led the Cougars to a second strafing of traditional power Arizona in two years. After Jimmer lit them up for 49 points as a junior, the Wildcats were primed to slow him down—and still couldn't. He scored 33 points and BYU won by 22.

"We killed them," Jimmer said. "It wasn't even a game. We killed this team that's a pretty good team and has some real good athletes. So I was thinking, 'Wow, we could be a *very* good team. We could be a team that is top five and makes a run in the NCAA tournament.' And I thought that right away, right after we won there.

"And then we played at UNLV three and a half weeks later. They were really good, and they were talking trash before the game. You know, all this stuff that went into it—we never have won there, and they always intimidated us. They thought they had it in the bag, and we came out there, determined as could be, and we beat them at their place. And I was thinking, 'This is going in the right direction, that's for sure, because that's a tough place to win for us.' We never had done that before, and we did it. It was easy to believe we were a special team and that this could be a special year."

The game that removed all doubt—and changed the arc of Jimmer's career—came near the end of January 2011. BYU hosted league rival San Diego State—undefeated, ranked No. 4 in the nation. The Cougars were 19–1 and ranked No. 9.

It was, by any measure, one of the biggest games in years for teams from outside the traditional power conferences. The matchup drew national media attention before, during, and especially after the game.

T. J. told Jimmer that a big victory and a big personal performance would make him "king of the world." Jimmer shrugged that off but understood the magnitude of the opportunity.

"Everyone was talking about it on every sports show, and you *knew* that everyone was going to be tuning in to watch that game," Jimmer said. "I knew it was a huge game for us. And I knew we could beat them because they're a good team, but they're the same San Diego State team that we played last year—same exact guys—and we knew how to beat them. And they were coming to our place, where they had struggled.

"So, we were confident, but we were definitely nervous because they were a good team and they had a lot of confidence coming in, but just the atmosphere was unbelievable. It was the craziest game I'd ever seen played at BYU by far. And just to see the fans—the arena was almost packed before we got out there. Even the older people who don't normally show up before ten minutes before the game, they were all there. The energy in the building and the signs and everything had the place rocking. It was an unbelievable experience.

"And then we got into the game, and you could feel the floor rumble because it was so loud in there. It was amazing. It really, really was. And I knew I was feeling it right from the beginning of the game."

This was the game that turned Jimmer into a certified phenomenon. This was the game, with the entire nation watching, in which Jimmer could not be stopped—scoring outside, scoring inside, scoring in splurges against a defense designed to thwart him.

He shot it from everywhere, and it went in. He drove fearlessly and got the ball into the basket. He got fouled and made his free throws.

When it was over, Jimmer had 43 of BYU's 71 points in a decisive Cougars victory. He had the Marriott Center crowd swarming him on the court, lifting him up, showering him with adulation. He had America eating out of the palm of his red-hot shooting hand.

Twitter blew up with hosannas to Jimmer. They came from NBA stars Kevin Durant and John Wall, from music stars such as the Red Hot Chili Peppers and Nelly, from media members nationwide. And in the arena it was even more intense—Jimmer facing an adoring mob and reflecting their ecstasy back at them, remembering his brother's pregame coronation message.

"I never had that happen before," he said. "It was exciting but also pretty scary. They were trying to lift me up and do all this different stuff. They were all just running at me.

"It was an unbelievable experience. It was hard to comprehend what we had just done. Everyone was so excited, and I thought to myself, 'Wow. Everyone just saw this performance. Everyone just saw us beat them, and I had a great game.'

"I didn't have Twitter at the time and didn't know much

about it, but my girlfriend did. She said to me, 'Jimmer, you don't *understand* what's going on right now. You're the number one trending topic. Everyone is tweeting about you.' I was thinking, 'What?' So I checked it out. That was when it started—'Jimmermania.'"

In the stands, T. J. Fredette—the guiding force for so many years—looked at a scene he might have dreamed but could scarcely believe.

"I don't think anyone was ready for that," T. J. said. "It was like a movie. I was in seventh heaven. My little brother was officially a rock star. My mother was telling me to go out on the floor and get him. 'He's going to get hurt,' she said. I just rolled my eyes and said, 'He's fine, Ma.'"

The sudden elevation of Jimmer's stature came with some collateral damage. After games, he would always go back out onto the court to spend time with Whitney and any family members who were at the game—but after the San Diego State game, that bonding time became impossible. Jimmer was pounced upon by autograph seekers and other fans, which meant he had to meet those closest to him at his apartment or at a restaurant.

Even going out to eat became an exercise in crowd management. Jimmer couldn't get ice cream at The Creamery on campus or eat dinner at the Olive Garden without drawing attention.

"His junior year, people would recognize him and say, 'It's Jimmer,' and that was it," T. J. said. "Every once in a while people would ask him for his autograph. It was the same way his senior year. Then after the San Diego State game, it was a total shift.

"He could no longer come out after games without getting mobbed. We'd go out to eat, and he'd get mobbed. He didn't know what to do. He never expected that. He was always confident in himself on the court, but the way the media grabbed hold of it and he got that cult following, I think that was tough for him to take. He had to learn to adapt and handle that."

But even rock stars have critics. As Jimmermania grew, he and BYU became both national darlings and cultural lightning rods. Most people loved Jimmer—except for those who deemed him an overhyped Great White Hope who shot too much, played defense too indifferently, and competed in an inferior conference.

The more the Cougars won and Jimmer scored, the less agreement there seemed to be on their star and their overall worth as a team. When they moved up to No. 1 in the RPI rankings and Jimmer took over the Player of the Year straw polling, critics turned up the volume on their doubts.

Entering the stretch run of a remarkable season, BYU might have been the most-discussed and most-debated team in the country, and Jimmer was definitely the most-discussed and most-debated player in the country.

Then the storyline abruptly and shockingly shifted.

With BYU roaring into March with a 27–2 record and as a serious contender for the national title, a bomb dropped. Brandon Davies, the Cougars' top rebounder and No. 3 scorer, was abruptly dismissed from the team for a BYU Honor Code violation.

As was subsequently reported and acknowledged by Davies, he had premarital sex with his girlfriend. After Davies admitted the violation to the Honor Code, the school's response was cut-and-dried—Davies' season was over. It didn't matter that the timing was cataclysmic for the basketball team; the school's famously strict code was more important than wins or losses.

On a Sunday night in Provo, Jimmer and his roommate, Charles Abouo, had a few people at their apartment, hanging out and savoring the Cougars' victory the day before at San Diego State—a victory that had clinched the Mountain West Conference title. That's when Charles whispered to him, "Hey, Jim, I need to talk to you real quick."

They went into the laundry room, and Charles told him what he'd just heard regarding Davies.

"I think something bad's going to happen to Brandon," Charles said. "I don't think he's going to able to play with us anymore. He did something wrong, and I think he's kicked out. I think he's gone."

Jimmer thought it was a joke at first, but the reality quickly dawned on him. This was no joke. He kept the devastating news to himself but was in shock all night.

"When Coach said it Monday, that's when I knew it was really true," Jimmer said. "I went through the two biggest emotional swings of my life. We had just beat San Diego State at their place. That was the second time we'd beat them, and that was *unbelievable* because their fans are crazy, and we went in there and shut them up again. And everyone was stunned. No one thought we were going to win that game. But we did it. Sunday went on and we were still really happy, and Monday hit and all of a sudden, we were at an *extreme* low."

Now shocked and vulnerable, BYU was routed in its next game by New Mexico, the only Mountain West Conference opponent it had lost to in the season.

"We just felt awful," Jimmer said. "You could tell those two days of practice weren't the same. They didn't feel the same. Even Coach was different. Everyone was different, just how mellow we were. How we just couldn't get it off our minds. And then Brandon—I just felt bad for Brandon. I didn't necessarily feel bad for our team as much as for him and his well-being, since he's such a good kid. But we went on to that game on Wednesday against New Mexico, still a packed crowd, everyone was excited because of what had just happened, going crazy—and then, the whole night was just off. The whole night, we got *killed*. We got beat by 20 points, and that never happens in the Marriott Center. It just felt like something was missing because Brandon wasn't there that game. He completely missed that game. He was home.

"After that game, we came together and said, 'Hey, we can't have that happen anymore.' It was terrible in the locker room. The biggest thing for us was that we invited Brandon to make sure that he was at every game with us. He started to sit on the bench, and it just started to make us feel better, make him feel better."

BYU basketball suddenly jumped the boundaries of sports and became a mainstream media topic. From CNN to Fox News to MSNBC, everyone was talking about Brandon Davies and the BYU Honor Code and what was right or wrong. Debate raged over whether BYU's Honor Code was hopelessly out of touch with today's cultural practices or a much-needed stand against growing permissiveness. All the major talk shows called both BYU and the Fredette family to try to get Jimmer on their shows to discuss it.

Despite the damage done to a dream season, Jimmer was adamant in his support of his school's decision.

"I was actually very proud of our school, and I was proud of Brandon and everybody who was involved," he said. "The girl went in and told what had happened, and Brandon didn't lie or anything. He confessed and said, 'Yup, that's what happened.' He faced the consequences, and the school did exactly what they should do.

"You have the contract, you have the code of conduct right there, and you sign it and you know what you're getting into as soon as you sign it. If you don't want to go to BYU and you don't want to live by those rules, don't go. But if you are going to go, you have to live by those rules. So, Brandon broke a rule, the code says what the consequences are, the school acted on it, and that's just the way it was. That's the way it happens.

"Again, I was extremely proud of my school for doing what it did because a lot of schools would have waited until after the season. A lot of schools wouldn't have even said anything, but I think people gained a lot of respect for BYU for handling it that way, especially in an era where there are lots of scandals going down. So, I think it was refreshing. Even though it hurt us, hurt him, hurt the team, hurt everybody involved, it was the right thing to do, and I was proud of us."

While the moral debate simmered, the only area of widespread agreement was that the flawed Cougars had no chance at accomplishing much without Davies. The ultimate goals were indeed no longer reachable, but there were some high points still to come.

The first came in the Mountain West Conference tournament semifinals in Las Vegas. BYU was matched up again with nemesis New Mexico, the team that had just flattened BYU a few days earlier in Provo, after Davies was suspended. The Lobos hadn't just swept the Cougars in 2011; they had beaten them six straight times.

Hardcore BYU fans approached Jimmer and told him they didn't believe the Cougars could win. As tip-off approached that night in Vegas, the generally laid-back Jimmer had shut himself off from his teammates, saying nothing to anyone. He was working himself into a cold fury.

"I'm not losing this game again," he told himself. "I can't lose to these guys one more time."

T. J. stoked the fire. Instead of the customary motivational pregame text, he called Jimmer and verbalized his message for added emphasis.

"Jimmer," T. J. said, "I want you to do whatever it takes to win this game. I don't care if you have to shut down their best player, if you have to get 15 rebounds, if you have to score 60."

He almost scored 60.

In what was the individual performance of the year nationally and probably the greatest individual game in Mountain West Conference history, Jimmer scorched New Mexico for 52 points.

He took 37 of BYU's 68 shots and had 22 of its 34 field goals. He scored the Cougars' first 10 points in less than three minutes and had 33 at halftime. Perhaps most remarkable of all, Jimmer did it almost exclusively the hard way—he shot just one free throw the entire night, scoring all the other 51 points from the field. As an added bonus, Jimmer passed BYU icon Danny Ainge as the leading scorer in school history.

When it was over and BYU finally had beaten New Mexico 87–76, the satisfaction was immense. A team most of the nation had given up on after the suspension of Davies showed it still had life left in it.

"I went nuts when we won that game. I was so happy," Jimmer said. "I didn't care what happened against San

Diego State—the next game—to be honest with you. I was *so* happy we won that game. I was like, '*That* was what I wanted to do! I don't care about this next game. Let's go to the tournament now. Let's go to the NCAA tournament.'"

BYU lost the next game to the Aztecs in the MWC final. The next night, the Cougars gathered to learn their NCAA destination and first-round opponent. The mood was tentative—how much, in terms of seeding, would the selection committee penalize BYU for the absence of Davies?

Jimmer feared the team could be dropped as low as a No. 6 or No. 7 seed, matching up against a formidable first-round opponent. But when the brackets were revealed, the Cougars were rewarded with a No. 3 seed—considered one of the top 12 teams in the 68-team tournament—and a trip to nearby Denver to play No. 14 seed Wofford College. Optimism returned in Provo.

"That was a great matchup for us, really," Jimmer said. "I was excited about it and I didn't even give a thought about losing that game. I was 100 percent sure we were going to win that game, and in the years past I didn't think that. But this one—I *knew* we had it in the bag as long we went out there and played well."

The Cougars did just that. After a slow start, Jimmer racked up 32 points, four rebounds, and seven assists. Then BYU awaited the winner of the St. John's-Gonzaga game that followed.

Jimmer was worried about facing St. John's University.

The Red Storm was a very good team from the powerful Big East Conference whose athletic players posed major matchup problems. But the plot line was altered when Gonzaga pounded St. John's, 86–71.

Gonzaga's win replaced one set of worries with another. BYU matched up better with Gonzaga, but the Zags were red-hot, having won their last nine games to make it to the NCAA tournament. After watching the team from Spokane throttle the Red Storm, the Cougars knew they would face a major challenge just 48 hours later.

This game would be a defining moment for the program—and for Jimmer's legacy. BYU hadn't advanced to the NCAA Sweet Sixteen since 1981, when Ainge was the hero. There had been so many early exits in the tournament—would this season, the finest in school history, add to that frustrating history? Or would the Cougars break through into a level reserved for the game's elite?

This time, Jimmer's supporting cast came through from the opening tip. He didn't attempt a shot for nearly six minutes and didn't score a point for more than eight minutes—and it didn't matter. By the time Jimmer finally made a shot, BYU had established that it was fully equal to the Gonzaga challenge.

Jimmer had 14 points at halftime and then pumped in 20 more during the second half in what became a rout. Gonzaga had no answer for the defensive wrinkle Dave Rose threw at them.

"We went into a zone defense, and they had no idea

what to do," Jimmer said. "It was amazing because against St. John's, Gonzaga looked unbelievably poised, really good against pressure. You know, got it up, found the open man, extra pass, bam, shot, perfect. We threw that zone at them and they just sat there. They didn't have an offense for it. The guys who had been so confident before, we would get into them, and they kind of didn't do anything.

"I was *so* happy after that game, 'cause that was one of the goals of my college career—to make it to the Sweet Sixteen. And to make it even better, no one thought we were going to win that game. It was gratifying to be able to do that and go into the second weekend knowing that we had a shot to keep playing. It was an exciting time for everybody at BYU."

Next stop: New Orleans and the Sweet Sixteen. As fate would have it, the opponent awaiting the Cougars was Florida, the team they had defeated in a double-overtime classic the previous year in the first round of the NCAA tourney.

That game had helped launch Jimmer's stardom— he had scored 37 points in a 99–92 BYU triumph. This time around, a more mature Gators team, carrying a No. 2 NCAA seeding, was obsessed with stopping the nation's leading scorer.

"I knew they were gunning for me," Jimmer said. After the season was over, Jimmer talked to Florida forward Chandler Parsons, who told him that in the days leading up to that game in New Orleans: "The *only* thing we talked about was Jimmer."

Swarmed by the Gators, Jimmer made just 11 of 29 shots and only 3 of 15 three-point attempts. It got worse as the game went along—Jimmer pulled a muscle in his calf just before halftime and played in pain from that point on. He also split open his chin while diving on the floor and had to have it stitched up. Despite the injuries, he played 44 out of 45 minutes in an overtime loss.

In the New Orleans stands, Kay Fredette felt her heart break a little bit. The Fredettes had gotten such joy out of watching their baby—all the successes, all the times he had surprised the doubters, all the times he had brought thousands of strangers to their feet. Suddenly, a dream season had ended.

"When he walked off the court after they lost to Florida in the NCAA tournament, I really felt it then," she said. "It truly was the last game of his college basketball career, and it was tough for me to see him walk off with a cut on his chin, limping from a sore calf muscle, and with a dejected look on his face. I wondered at that time what he was feeling and whether he realized that it was the very last game that he would play in his college career. I never did ask him, but Jimmer being Jimmer, he just takes things in stride more than his mother does, I guess."

He did take it in stride—as much as possible. But it still hurt. The physical pain from the injuries was one thing, but the emotional pain from the frustrating closure of the last chapter in his college basketball life was greater.

"What a way to go out, you know what I mean?" Jimmer said. "We still had our chances, though, that was the thing. We went into overtime. We didn't make a couple of plays at the end and lost the game, but it was definitely a good effort. And I remember walking off the court, all bandaged and bruised, and thinking, 'You know, it was a great run, but this is it.' And it's crazy how it just ends. You're so excited, you know, and then it just ends."

Despite the disappointment of that ending, it was a season of triumph for the program and for Jimmer. He swept up Player of the Year honors from coast to coast before facing the final frontier of doubters: the NBA.

CHAPTER TWELVE

RACE

When Jimmer's senior season ended, his tour of the awards circuit began. Everywhere he turned, someone wanted to give him some hardware. He won Player of the Year awards named for Dr. James Naismith (inventor of the game of basketball), John Wooden (winner of a record 10 national championships), and Oscar Robertson (arguably the most versatile player in college basketball history). Among others.

Hauling in all that loot necessitated a trip to Houston for the Final Four. Given the painful nature of BYU's ouster the week before, Jimmer's heart really wasn't into that whole scene.

"They asked me if I wanted to go to the games," Jimmer recalled. "I said, 'Nah, I'm all right.' And I didn't even really watch much of it on TV. I watched some of the national championship game, actually. It was not a great game."

Connecticut beat Butler in the title game, 55–42. The overmatched Bulldogs, who reached the Final Four by beating the Florida team that had eliminated BYU, put on one of the worst offensive displays in the history of the NCAA tournament.

"That made it hurt even worse because we could have easily been there," Jimmer said. "We had the path, but it just doesn't happen sometimes. . . . If Brandon had played, I *knew* it would have been different. But we could have made it there even without him, because we had Butler next and they're a good team, but we could have beat Butler. And then it would have been the Final Four, and we would have had VCU [Virginia Commonwealth University, the team Butler beat handily to reach the title game]. So, it definitely was set up—even without Brandon. But if we had had Brandon, I think we could have *really* done some damage."

Eventually, though, it was time to shelve the what-ifs and move on. Jimmer is good at that—in fact, he is better at it than most. After the Final Four, it was time to prepare for the next stage in his basketball odyssey—the NBA draft.

As Jimmer dived into preparation, the media accelerated its draft speculation. Among the hotter topics, though it was rarely spelled out this bluntly, was this: Is Jimmer too white to play in the NBA?

It wasn't the first time a Fredette had been questioned about the role of race in his career choice.

In the course of conversations with those who don't know her well, Lindsay Fredette-Peterson occasionally will be asked what her brothers do for a living. Her answers almost always produce looks of surprise and confusion—even outright suspicion, as if she's making a joke or pulling a prank.

T. J. raps, she tells them. No, not gifts. He writes and performs hip-hop songs.

And baby brother Jimmer? He plays in the National Basketball Association.

"It's just something people aren't expecting," she says.

The first reason people aren't expecting that answer is literally skin-deep. A white rapper? A white NBA player? Really?

Both brothers have entered entertainment genres that are dominated by African-Americans. White people are huge consumers of both hip-hop music and pro basketball—but not many of them are performers in those fields. And white people who attempt to make it big in either hip-hop or professional hoops face a society full of doubters.

America has made vast progress in race relations over the years, but we do not yet live in a color-blind society. When racial curiosities such as Jimmer and T. J. present themselves, people tend to notice—and talk about it.

The Fredette brothers would love to be viewed beyond skin color. Though T. J. no longer aspires to a career in hip-hop, he still pursues the art form as a hobby. He enjoys writing lyrics and putting songs together, but that's about it now. Even so, the brothers would love to be judged on their abilities with a basketball or a microphone without any racial considerations. They try not to listen or pay attention to criticism or doubters, but they know what's been said about them:

They're posers. They're inauthentic. They can't possibly be good enough.

The Fredette demographics seem to further skew the odds against the boys. They're from Glens Falls, New York, a town that according to 2010 census numbers is 93.3 percent white and 1.6 percent black. And they are members of the LDS church. Though religious affiliation certainly doesn't preclude them from either career, it further emphasizes their minority status.

But don't try to tell T. J. he can't be a practicing Latter-day Saint and a rapper at the same time. And do not use the phrase "Mormon rapper" in his presence.

"That makes it sound as though I'm rapping about Mormon doctrine," T. J. said. "I'm not. I'm sure there've been hip-hop artists who were Catholics or Baptists or whatever, and I don't hear anybody bringing that up.

"I come from a much different background than most rappers. I started rapping with a lot of kids who were from tough environments, from the ghettos, but because of major differences in lyrical content, it didn't work out. That's when I went on my own and started writing solo.

"You don't have to be from the ghetto to write a rap song. Everyone in this life has stories and experiences. It doesn't have to be about drugs and the ghetto to be a good rap song. Once people hear me, they see I have a good sound, and it's not corny. I write good metaphors." There was a long stream of white rappers that were not quite taken seriously, an aspersion that didn't really change until Eminem crashed the scene.

Eminem—whose real name is Marshall Mathers—came out of Detroit in the late '90s as a breakthrough white hip-hop artist who went big. In Glens Falls, T. J. Fredette took notice. He listened to several East Coast rappers—Nas, Biggie Smalls, Wu-Tang Clan—but also felt an affinity to Eminem.

In spite of his race, Eminem went on to almost universal critical and commercial success and has been embraced throughout the African-American hip-hop culture. T. J. was hoping to ride that wave in recent years, but his aspirations have changed since then. He no longer wants to perform, but he would like to transition to other things that involve writing. His very creative mind keeps him awake nights thinking of ideas and ways to break into other avenues of writing. He has written a screenplay and hopes to one day see it on the big screen.

"I was not a sideshow," he said. "I was doing this for a long time before Jimmer became famous. I enjoyed the performing, and I was good at what I did, but I want to move on from that now."

Jimmer was good at what he did, too. But the doubt-ers were everywhere. He graduated from a largely white high school. Then he came out of the whitest of college environments—about 1.1 percent of BYU's student body in 2010–11 was African-American, and only a couple of his basketball teammates were black. The Ultimate White Guy found himself trying to convince the NBA he had the chops to play in a league dominated by black players.

The NBA had been that way for a while already. In 1997, around the time Jimmer first took up competitive basketball, *Sports Illustrated* published a cover story en-titled, "What Ever Happened to the White Athlete?" The provocative article documented the "white flight" from mainstream sports, discussed the reasons why, and pre-dicted that the trend would not be reversed anytime soon:

"The white athlete is getting out. The white athlete—and here we speak of the young men in team sports who ruled the American athletic scene for much of the cen-tury—doesn't want to play anymore. Distracted by other leisure-time pursuits and discouraged by the success of black athletes, who have come to dominate sports in spec-tacular fashion, the white athlete is now less interested in playing certain mainstream games, most notably basket-ball and football, than are his black counterparts. He is in-creasingly drawn to sports that in the U.S. are played pri-marily by whites, such as soccer, or to alternative athletic pursuits that are overwhelmingly white, such as mountain biking or rock climbing. After a six-month *Sports Illustrated* inquiry into the subject of race and sports, including dozens of interviews with coaches, athletes, executives, and academics and a nationwide poll of 1,835 middle school and high school kids, all indications are that the white athlete will continue his steady fade."

Statistics bear that out. In the early 1990s, roughly 25 percent of NBA roster spots belonged to American-born white players. According to ESPN.com, that number dwindled to about 12 percent in 2011–12, Jimmer's first year as a pro. At the very time he was entering the league, it was trending farther away than ever from players who looked like him.

After leaving BYU, Jimmer was trying to become the first American-born white guard drafted in the top 10 since Kirk Hinrich in 2003. Besides Hinrich and Jimmer, these are your white American top-10 picks (all of them forwards or centers): Gordon Hayward, Joe Alexander, Kevin Love, Spencer Hawes, Adam Morrison, and Luke Jackson.

Kevin Love has been a great success in Minnesota, leading the league in rebounding in 2010–11 and being named the NBA's Most Improved Player. Hawes has been a starter for most of his five-year career. Hayward became a starter on the Utah Jazz team in his second year, 2011–12.

The other three have done next to nothing. They have combined to make just 31 career starts and were not on active NBA rosters in 2010–11.

Given that spotty production for high draft picks,

everyone in the world of professional hoops was furiously debating whether Jimmer was an overhyped Great White Hope or had legitimate NBA star potential. Every ESPN opinion show did segments parsing Jimmer's game and arguing over his potential. Sometimes they came straight out and mentioned race; more often that was the unspoken undercurrent of the discussion.

Of course, this was just a louder and more national version of the knocks Jimmer took during the college recruiting process. He was a scoring machine in high school, but scouts questioned then whether he would fare well against the quicker, bigger players in college. He answered that by winning seven national Player of the Year awards as a senior at BYU.

Actually, he'd used racial typecasting to his advantage for years. When playing on the racially mixed Albany City Rocks AAU team, Jimmer was often pegged by opponents as a nonplayer. Either that or as a one-dimensional player, who could only catch and shoot. When he turned out to be the best player on the team, the joke was on those who had underestimated him.

The same was true at BYU and had been for years before Jimmer arrived. One look at the Cougars on film or in layup lines, and it was easy for some opponents to think those (white) guys were overmatched.

From the 1997 *Sports Illustrated* article: "The Cougars have defeated black teams that started games thinking that when push came to shove, their own athletic superiority would tell. San Diego Padres outfielder Tony Gwynn learned this. As a junior point guard in 1980 he went to Provo, Utah, with his San Diego State team and got beaten badly. 'Those BYU guys were flying through the air, jumping over guys, getting rebounds, and that's the first time I thought, These guys are really athletic,' Gwynn says. 'Our whole club was shocked.'

"The next day someone tried to soothe Gwynn's pain by saying that the Cougars had special springs under their floor. 'We're like, Aw, no wonder! I knew they couldn't jump!' Gwynn says with a laugh. Only later did he realize: 'How come I wasn't jumping any higher?'"

Among the shockingly athletic white kids playing for BYU at that time was star guard Danny Ainge, the guy who held the school scoring record until Jimmer broke it. As an executive with the Boston Celtics, Ainge had counseled Jimmer to enjoy his senior season in college, and his words had rung true. He also believed in Jimmer as a pro—but the NBA cognoscenti were split.

They wanted to know whether Jimmer was going to be the next Adam Morrison—a national Player of the Year at Gonzaga who was drafted second overall and bombed in the NBA—or the next Ainge. Ainge was the BYU hero in the early 1980s who became a two-sport professional athlete, playing baseball and basketball, in which he became a backcourt fixture with some world championship Celtics teams.

The usual racial buzzwords came into play whenever

Jimmer's name came up: Is he "athletic" enough to play in the NBA? (Read: black.) Or will he have to rely on his "basketball IQ" to get by? (Read: white.)

Jimmer didn't want to talk about race, but the sports world would not stop asking about it. It came up during his guest spot on *Pardon the Interruption,* the popular and influential ESPN show starring Tony Kornheiser and Michael Wilbon. It came up during interviews in New York on the eve of the draft. The topic followed him everywhere.

"In some people's minds, I think, it has somewhat of an effect sometimes," Jimmer said. "But it shouldn't. If you can play basketball, you can play basketball. But I don't want to accuse anybody.

"It's all good. I hope they just see the basketball player and see what I can do on the floor. I don't think the color of someone's skin has anything to do with it."

Jimmer could show skeptics the *Sports Illustrated* cover from March 2011, which displayed his leaping ability as he lifted off for a jump shot against Gonzaga. But more important, he needed to showcase his athleticism during the individual team workouts he attended and when he was tested at the NBA combine.

Jimmer busted a few stereotypes and preconceived notions in those venues. He was measured at 6 feet, 2 inches and 196 pounds, with 7.7 percent body fat. He bench-pressed 185 pounds 14 times, a good number for a point guard. Most important, he completed the agility test in good time, faster than Kentucky's Brandon Knight, among others, and ran well in the three-quarter-court sprint. The only athletic measurement that left him appreciably behind his peers was his vertical leap: he had a 28-inch jump without a step and 33 inches with one step.

"Every coach I talked to said, 'Wow, you are more athletic than I thought you were. You are quicker,'" Jimmer recalls. "I went to the NBA-sponsored workouts and showed them. I went to the combine and tested really well, tested as one of the most athletic guys at the combine."

This was a tip of the hat to all the training done with his uncle Lee, who spent all those years working to maximize Jimmer's quickness, explosiveness, balance, and coordination. The time in the garage, in the gym, and in the driveway had paid off. Though there were still going to be concerns about his ability to defend NBA-level guards, Jimmer had proved he was not flat-out overmatched physically. There was no doubt, after the combine, that Jimmer would be a first-round pick and most likely a lottery pick, which would be one of the top 14 selections.

Needless to say, his family was not surprised. They'd been watching Jimmer turn doubters into believers for years.

"He can't score the way he scores and get to the rim the way he does without being athletic," T. J. said. "He's had some of the most athletic guys in the country guarding him, and he could still get to the rim. It's something you've just got to deal with, to keep showing them."

Jimmer helped his draft stock away from the court as well with the in-person interviews at each franchise workout. He had no red flags in his background—no failed drug tests, no concerns about substance abuse, no legal issues, no negative reports from school officials.

That's big. Teams that are handing millions of dollars to young men from a variety of backgrounds have to do their homework to make sure they're not throwing away cash on a bad investment. Background checks are done on all the top prospects.

If any were done on Jimmer, they came back remarkably bland. His clean living had its rewards. He was a no-risk draftee in terms of personal character and comportment.

Jimmer came in so drama-free that the topic he heard about most from scouts was what happened with Brandon Davies' suspension at BYU. Some front-office execs just wanted to know the behind-the-scenes gossip of what really happened.

When the questions got around to basketball, he was more than ready to showcase his knowledge. Show Jimmer some film and he knew what he was looking at. Ask him to draw a play or a defense on a grease board and it wasn't a problem. The lifelong basketball junkie loved sitting down with Indiana Pacers' president and legendary player Larry Bird to talk hoops.

Jimmer was so prepared for the interviews, so well-versed and grounded, that one unnamed, long-time general manager told Yahoo! Sports NBA writer Adrian Wojnarowski that Jimmer was the most impressive interview he'd ever had.

"Most of the interviewers kind of knew who I was, and they knew what I stood for," Jimmer said. "A lot of them would say, 'I don't really know what to ask you because you don't have anything wrong with you.' So they would just kind of ask about basketball.

"I took a psychological test during one interview. But most of the time, the teams talked about my family, about BYU, about what I felt about playing in the NBA, what I wanted to play, how I'd fit in with their team—those types of questions. With some guys, I guess they grill them and ask them about things that they'd been through. But I didn't have too much of that."

As the process ground on, T. J. was moved to write a song he called "The Grand Finale."

This whole thing is like a Rocky movie
It takes a lot to move me
But I've been moved and inspired we
Got a lot to prove we
Just touched the surface of the purpose we've
    been working for
We heard the roar of the crowds that cheer
But now we're working more
We've just started
The haters talking garbage

THE CONTRACT

The newspapers better buy an extra ink cartridge
Because the press is impressed
Now they're loving it
They're coming with cameras in hand
So they can cover it
And once they get a taste of it
Its greatness in the making
No mistaking
It's all within grasp, time for taking it
You made it kid and most impressive is the way
you did it
Took the little gift you were given and then you
made it big
Behind the scenes I told 'em that your grind was
mean
We let 'em know what it is
Never hide the dream
We're almost at the top and dropping's not an
option
A lot of goals that were close now we finally got
them
Honestly I'm honored to witness it no one can
stop them
We get the picture now the opening comes
I know you'll find the seam
Find a team
Live out your dream
Never mind the cream

RACE

The world's gone is the message
Staying aggressive
Not allowing anybody to mess with
What you sweated it for
Now we're out for getting more
Step in the door ready for war
Reaching the goal already in store
Happens fast it's becoming a reality
The grand finale and rallies
It's in-line with another galaxy
No longer is it fantasy
This was planned to be
And granted we're excited but this didn't happen
    randomly
It was the preparation
It was the expectation
You made it happen now the cities need a nation
So I'll explain it
It was desire mixed with dedication
Instead of waiting you went after it
And set the stage something so amazing
Now the greatness is about to blossom
Now the stakes have been rising
History in the making
It's the grand finale
And yes it's amazing
We're getting so close now
It's there for the taking

THE CONTRACT

Got him anxiously awaiting
Oh yes it's so amazing.

By late June 2011, it was all over but the guesswork. Finally, on a summer night in New Jersey, The Contract would be fulfilled and Jimmer would be a pro. But that day of destiny would only be the beginning of a long, strange journey to the final reward.

CHAPTER THIRTEEN

DREAM

David Stern, the commissioner of the NBA, was at the podium in the Majestic Ballroom on the fifth floor of the Westin Times Square Hotel. It was early afternoon on June 23, 2011—draft day. Arrayed around Stern were 17 young men who would hear their names called that night in the first round of the draft. The first step of their nascent professional careers would be to cross a stage and shake Stern's hand as a new member of an NBA team.

This was, by any definition, a power lunch. High-profile agents sat with nervous young clients and their families. The room was packed with current and future millionaires from around the nation and around the globe.

Stern had a microphone in his hand and was speaking in his smooth New York patois, welcoming the players and their families. Just as he was getting going, a lone voice rang out from the otherwise rapt audience.

Jason Peterson, Jimmer's two-year-old nephew, loudly piped up while wandering away from the family table. The only person in the room not awed to be in the company of the commissioner had no interest in keeping quiet.

While Jason shouted, Stern attempted to keep his welcome speech on track. When that was futile, he cracked a joke about it.

"All right, make a note," he said into the microphone. "It's the Jimmer table."

The Jimmer table was already unique in the room. There was no coffee at any of the eight places, just apple juice and water. Some tables were flush with men in power suits, but the attire was more casual for the Fredettes—jeans for T. J., a polo shirt for Al. Conversation flowed easily, whereas other tables were quiet and tense. And then little Jason Peterson piped up and made his presence known to David Stern.

Part of being a Fredette is having the close-knit family together whenever possible—even if that means risking interrupting one of the most powerful figures in the sports world. Jimmer's sister, Lindsay, handed off her month-old son, Ty, to her husband, Brent, and swooped in to grab Jason. She whisked him (kicking and screaming) out of the ballroom, restoring order.

"I was so embarrassed," Brent said when the lunch was over.

"It's always something," said Al Fredette, more amused

than annoyed at another laugh-track moment in the colorful family history.

That was the first hitch in the draft-day plan. It would not be the last.

After lunch, the Fredettes retired to the lounge area on the ninth floor and tried to get a final handle on draft logistics. The last of 46 tickets for friends and family were dispersed. Hotel keys were lost and recovered. Watches were synchronized for the bus trip the NBA arranged for families from the Westin to the Prudential Center in New Jersey, site of the draft. A succession of friends, acquaintances, and NBA staff floated in and out to wave hello, say good luck, beg an autograph, snap a picture with Jimmer, or ask if the family needed anything during the seemingly interminable wait.

Among the visitors was Tyson Poulos, a friend from Glens Falls who as an adolescent was one of the many extended-stay residents of the basement at 26 Ogden Street. When Tyson's mother died, Al Fredette had stepped in as a strong parental figure to the young boy.

Wearing baggy jeans, hightops, a silver medallion necklace, suit coat, and tie, Tyson stopped by the hotel to pay his respects. He now lived in the city and proudly told Al and Kay Fredette that he was enrolled in college—news that pleased Al immensely.

"They're the greatest people I've ever known in my life," Tyson said. "I was baptized by Al into the church when I was eight. Anything I've asked him, Al helped me out with. I've never found a nicer family."

Tyson brought with him a copy of the *New York Post,* with a headline that read, "Jimmer Debate Enlivens Dull Draft."

Since draft coverage is now a cottage industry in sports media, the "Jimmer Debate" had an extensive—even exhaustive—run through the spring of 2011 and right up to June 22. That debate helped fuel more than 2.2 million page views in twenty days at FollowJimmer.com, a personal YouTube site that featured documentary footage from a Tupelo Honey Productions film crew that followed him throughout his preparations for the draft. After each of his workouts with five teams—Sacramento, Utah, Phoenix, Indiana, and New York—the media in those cities weighed the pros and cons of Jimmer. And when the NBA made players available to the media the day before the draft, that debate helped bring by far the biggest crowd of reporters to Jimmer's table.

"I just want to show people out there you can make it from anywhere," Jimmer told them.

At the luncheon, Stern had congratulated the assembled draftees on exactly that—making it to this moment from all kinds of backgrounds and circumstances. "It's a pretty big miracle to be here," he said and delivered a talk that combined advice, encouragement, and marching orders.

"You're going to be judged by your worst moment, not

your best moment," Stern said. He told the players they were obligated to be leaders and to understand their social responsibility as such, so that they could leave a positive imprint on their communities. He exhorted them to celebrate safely that night. He gently needled Texas big man Tristan Thompson for being late to a players' meeting that morning with NBA officials.

And he encouraged them to take ownership of the growth of the sport.

"It's your game," he said.

Then Stern touched on the subject that was in the back of every mind in the room: the league's collective bargaining agreement and the looming lockout. As exciting as draft day was for all of them, a lockout could keep them from signing contracts and earning a fabulous living.

"You have a good union," Stern said. "I've been dealing with that union since 1966 . . . I don't know what will happen, but you can't go wrong being informed and aware."

That foreshadowed a lengthy lockout that pitted players against owners in a contentious battle to shape the future of the league. The rookies were largely just helpless bystanders as negotiations dragged on and games were canceled.

But for Jimmer, a few more months without an NBA paycheck was not going to be the end of the world. He'd never been rich before, and he wasn't rushing into an opulent lifestyle.

"I don't need anything," he said. "I'm not a guy who's grown up with a lot of stuff. We had our friendships and sports, and that's basically what we did. My parents bought things for me, but I preferred wearing T. J.'s big T-shirts. There are pictures of me when I was a kid, wearing shirts that would come past my knees. They were always tournament shirts that he won. So I had no concern about what I wore."

On the cusp of his professional career, the only things he wished for were a tropical vacation—"One of those places with white beaches and the water is almost aqua or greenish, a real nice color"—and a nice house.

"I always wanted a big house," he said. "Our house is really small, and none of my friends had big houses. When I went to a big house out of state or something, I loved it. You could run around. You can't run in our house.

"It won't be huge, but it will be big to me. One I can run around in."

After briefly mingling with friends and family in the ninth-floor lounge, it was time for Jimmer to flee the draft-related tumult for his hotel room and whatever rest his nerves would allow. He'd spent several exhausting weeks as the lightning rod of the draft. Now a lifetime goal was so near he could almost touch it.

Jimmer had already given the family his breakdown of what he thought would happen. He expected to be taken between 12 and 17, though trades could change that. And sure enough, by the time the Fredettes had taken the bus through the Holland Tunnel to Newark and arrived at the Prudential Center for the draft, a trade had already occurred.

Sacramento, one of the teams that worked out Jimmer individually, moved down from No. 7 to No. 10. Jimmer and his Octagon agent, Chris Emens, took that as a sign that the Kings were interested in him with that tenth pick.

Jimmer had loved his Sacramento workout. Owners Joe and Gavin Maloof told him they'd been fans of his for years. General manager Geoff Petrie loved scorers. Coach Paul Westphal and Jimmer hit it off well.

If Sacramento was to be the spot, the Fredettes would be fine with that. And especially fine, after all the debate and the criticisms, with being a top-10 pick.

When it was time to report to the green room on the floor of the Prudential Center, Jimmer had T. J., his mom and dad, BYU coach Dave Rose, and Emens in tow. It was a brutally difficult decision on who would get the five seats, and Jimmer was sorry to leave his longtime girl-friend, Whitney, out of the group.

Whitney sat 14 rows off the floor in the stands with her mother and brother and many of Jimmer's relatives. She knew the excitement of the night would be comple-mented by an equally large feeling of relief. At last Jimmer would know where his future path would lead him.

"It wore on him," she said of the draft process. "He was pretty dead. Every night I got a text from him saying, 'I can't wait for this to be over.'"

It was getting close.

In another section of the Prudential Center sat a group of friends wearing red-and-black Glens Falls High School gear with No. 32 on it—Jimmer's number. A second group of lifelong friends was one more section over. No draftee had a bigger group of supporters.

Back home in Glens Falls, they closed Angelina's for the night, since most of the ownership and work force had gone to Jersey for the draft. The Tupelo Honey film crew had grabbed a few of Jimmer's friends and gotten them to individually voice their pride and excitement for him and Kate Foley, the client manager, showed Jimmer a two-minute clip that brought tears to his eyes.

"Hopefully when he gets called there will be a good roar in the crowd," T. J. said.

There were plenty of other Jimmer fans in the house, too. That included a group of six adolescent boys from Montville, New Jersey, wearing white T-shirts that together spelled out J-I-M-M-E-R.

"He's amazing," said Alex Olympio, one of the six, unknowingly invoking the title of T. J.'s rap song about Jimmer.

Wearing a navy blue suit, light blue tie, and blue gingham shirt with white collar, Jimmer entered the Green Room with his entourage and made his way to his assigned table. To his right sat T. J., the brother who had been his right-hand man for so long now.

"He's still the same kid he was in Glens Falls," Whitney Wonnacott said. "He just dresses better."

A three-foot-high railing draped with black curtains was all that separated the players from the media on the floor of the arena. The players were otherwise exposed to the fans in the stands, who could watch their every move and reaction. It was a very public way to have your future unfold.

Shortly after the ESPN telecast began at 7 P.M., host Stuart Scott worked his way through his opening script to a question that brought a loud response from the Prudential Center crowd: "And where will Jimmer go?"

Roughly 90 minutes later, the world found out. To Sacramento, as suspected, though it wasn't quite that simple.

As part of an ESPN draft promo that was taped earlier, several players were featured in old-school outfits "playing" jazz instruments. Jimmer, dressed in a cardigan sweater and tweed ivy cap, dutifully tapped at a drum kit. That was shown on the big screen, followed by a shot of Jimmer in the Green Room, followed by a Jay Bilas breakdown of Jimmer as an NBA prospect.

Bilas was 90 percent positive in his review but repeated the recurring concern among doubters: "He's going to have to guard in the NBA. Teams are going to go after him hard."

The draft began predictably, with Duke freshman point guard Kyrie Irving chosen first by Cleveland. That was followed by a less-anticipated run on big men: first Arizona's Derrick Williams to Minnesota, then Enes Kanter of Turkey (by way of Kentucky, where he never played) to Utah. Then the ESPN cameras found Jimmer, as the announcers discussed him as a possible Utah Jazz selection with their second pick of the first round at No. 12.

Jimmer laughed. The fans cheered. The anticipation was building.

The next three picks were all big men as well: Tristan Thompson of Texas was the surprise fourth overall pick, to Cleveland; Toronto selected Lithuanian center Jonas Valanciunas; and the Washington Wizards took forward Jan Vesely. The crowd erupted when Vesely gave his statuesque girlfriend a Hollywood smooch in the Green Room, and Jimmer caught Whitney's eyes in the stands and laughed.

At No. 7, Sacramento was technically on the clock—but it was selecting for the Charlotte Bobcats, who had traded up for the pick. Sacramento was the first of the teams projected as a likely landing spot for Jimmer—ESPN's Andy Katz had reported on that early in the draft broadcast—and his face filled the Prudential Center big screen. The Kings selected power forward Bismack Biyombo from the Congo, which surprised nobody at the Fredette table. They were waiting for the call at No. 10.

Then, finally, it was time for the point guards to be picked. Kentucky's Brandon Knight, a presumed top-five pick, went eighth to Detroit. And when Connecticut point guard Kemba Walker was taken with the ninth pick, T. J. turned to Jimmer with raised eyebrows and a look that said, "You're next."

In the small eternity it took for Stern to return to the podium and announce the pick, nobody said anything at the Jimmer table. They sat in silence. T. J. rubbed his chin and swallowed hard. Jimmer clenched his jaw. Then suddenly the tell-tale ESPN and NBATV cameras hovered around the table, Stern said the words, and before he knew it Jimmer was on his feet as the arena erupted.

The first thing Jimmer did was turn to his right and hug T. J.—the ultimate believer and the brother who had been there coaching him, cajoling him, encouraging him, pushing him for so many years. The brother who had also struggled so badly, drawing on Jimmer's success for inspiration. The brother who had made it through the worst times, emerging more healthy and happy than he'd been in years—able now to play some pickup ball, to travel, to be there and appreciate this dream come true.

"He just said, 'You did it,' when we hugged," Jimmer recalled.

It was a brief but powerful moment.

Then Jimmer hugged Kay, then Dave Rose, then Al. Then a Milwaukee Bucks hat was on his head—until the trade to Sacramento was official, Jimmer had to be announced and introduced as a Milwaukee selection.

The handshake with Stern happened in something of a fog. For Stern it was likely just another routine handshake with another player coming into the league. For Jimmer, it was a dreamed-about moment that came and went so quickly it was hard for him to latch onto it. At the family table in the Green Room, though, T. J. was struck by a momentary jolt of perspective.

"When he got up there taking the picture with David Stern, shaking his hand, it gave me chills," T. J. said. "Everything raced through my mind all at once—all we went through to get there. There was a brief moment of that."

Then T. J. had to tend to the explosion of texts and phone calls from friends and family members. He was in charge of accepting all congratulations and then directing all the Jimmer supporters in the arena to the family after-party.

"I just wanted to make sure everything went smoothly for the family," he said.

After the grip-and-grin with Stern, Jimmer was escorted offstage for an interview with ESPN reporter Mark Jones. While waiting for the interview, Jimmer waved to a smiling Whitney, his family up in the stands, and then to the Glens Falls crew. On the big screen, they showed the Jimmer Jam celebration at the Glens Falls Civic Center, and Jimmer's eyes glistened for a moment as he looked up and watched his hometown happily celebrating.

Then suddenly Jimmer was his customarily composed self as Jones asked his questions. That was followed by ESPN reporter Heather Cox interviewing T. J. about their bond. After an ESPN Radio interview, Jimmer was escorted off the floor of the arena and into what was called the Player Phone Room, located under the stands of the Prudential Center.

Most everyone thought Jimmer would be there for a few minutes, until the trade was approved by the NBA office and made official. He wound up staying in the room for more than two hours, getting his first experience with the red tape of pro sports.

In the process of vetting the trade, the NBA's legal team had to look into some whispers that Bismack Biyombo was not really nineteen, the minimum age to be drafted. The process wound up taking forever.

Meanwhile, the Fredette family and friends excitedly adjourned to the party they had arranged at the nearby Westminster Hotel, not knowing about the investigation that was going on back at the Prudential Center. The marathon vetting session dragged on, sapping a good deal of the fun from the night.

"That was kind of annoying, to be honest," Jimmer said. "Because I wanted to share the moment with everybody, but I couldn't."

While Jimmer sat around with nothing to do but contemplate his future and wonder how the party was progressing at the Westminster, Coach Rose appeared in the Prudential Center back hallway looking very proud.

"This is really a unique experience," he said. "You always want your players to graduate and go on and play professionally, but to be picked in the best league in the world, with one of the top picks, is an amazing accomplishment. I just kept saying, 'Wow, this is unbelievable.' The people in Sacramento are getting a guy they're going to love to watch."

After Jimmer was finally released from NBA purgatory—this time with a purple Sacramento Kings hat on his head—he still had to run the media gauntlet. He sat before the print and online media, answering questions. Then he did an array of live television interviews for outlets with specific local Jimmer interest—upstate New York, Utah, and California. He managed to give his father a brief hug before being rushed to an ESPN.com live chat, where he answered six questions before being moved again.

There were more TV hits, then a Sirius Radio interview, and a one-on-one with TNT's Craig Sager. Sager scored points by giving Jimmer a plate of Dirt Dogs—chili dogs from Dirty John's on South Street in Glens Falls. Al Fredette, who hadn't eaten since that lunch with Stern, inhaled three of them in rapid succession.

The interviews kept coming. A Sacramento outfit asked Jimmer to tape a couple of promos. He got the first one: "Hey, Sacramento, I'm Jimmer Fredette. Be heard!" On the second one, he said, "Hey, Jimmer Fredette, I'm Sacramento . . ." causing everyone to break up laughing. It was about midnight, and everyone was mentally fried—the draft pick included.

While traversing the back hallways of the Prudential

Center, Octagon reps Chris Emens and Kate Foley peppered Jimmer with questions while making travel arrangements to Sacramento the following day. Between obligations, he had to pick a jersey number on the fly—32 was taken by Francisco Garcia, and the only other number he'd ever worn, No. 5, was taken by Pooh Jeter. Foley gave him a couple of options: 25 and 37. She suggested 37, since it is the sum of 32 and 5. A little later Jimmer was asked one last time what number he wanted so the Kings could print jerseys for the press conference. His final answer was 7. Jimmer Fredette would be number 7 of the Sacramento Kings.

"I was excited, but I was also really scared and nervous because I didn't know what was ahead of me," Jimmer said. "You know, you're going to a new city, you don't know anybody. You don't know your teammates, you don't know what they're like. You don't know what the system's like. You don't know if you're going to play well. You don't know anything. So, it's really different, going out there on your own. It's definitely very, very scary. I never thought I would feel that way. I thought it would just be like pure joy, pure excitement, but it's definitely not like that. It's a feeling that's hard to describe, that's for sure."

At 12:15 A.M., after the ESPN talent had left the building, Jimmer's final duty was to have his picture taken by the NBA in his Kings hat and holding a Kings ball. Jimmer smiled broadly for several pictures. Nearby, an NBA communications worker who had followed the entire carnival murmured, "That poor kid."

At 12:20, it was done. Jimmer had missed his own draft party. Friends and family had converged at the Westminster shortly after he was selected, and a special creation from the Cake Boss TV show people had been brought in. But the delay in making the trade official made it impossible for Jimmer to get there and see everyone.

All that was left to do was get on the player bus back to Manhattan, agent and dad in tow, tie still knotted tightly around his neck, eyes glazed. He was the last player out of the Prudential Center.

So, at 12:25 in the morning of June 24, 2011, an exhilarated but exhausted Jimmer Fredette closed down the NBA draft and a chapter in his life. Two decades of personal dedication and familial investment, of belief in the face of doubt, of perseverance when confronted by obstacles, of striving instead of quitting, had gotten him here, to this place. The setting was just a few hours from where he spent his boyhood but also light-years removed from that small house in a small town in upstate New York where a boy and his big brother had dared to dream of this day.

He was too tired and stressed in the moment to see it, but everything was now laid out in front of him.

Jimmer walked out into the warm New Jersey night and boarded the bus. Next stop, the future.